Tiki Barber

ALL-PRO ON AND OFF THE FIELD

by Tom Needham

Enslow Publishers, Inc.
40 Industrial Road
Box 398
Berkeley Heights, NJ 07922
USA
http://www.enslow.com

Library of Congress Cataloging-in-Publication Data
Needham, Tom.
  Tiki Barber : all-pro on and off the field / by Tom Needham.
    p. cm. — (Sports stars with heart)
  Includes bibliographical references and index.
  ISBN-13: 978-0-7660-2865-4
  ISBN-10: 0-7660-2865-8
  1. Barber, Tiki, 1975—Juvenile literature. 2. Football players—United States—Biography—Juvenile literature. 3. New York Giants (Football team)—Juvenile literature.
  GV939.B37N44 2007
  796.332092—dc22
  [B]   2006031920

Credits
Editorial Direction: Red Line Editorial, Inc. (Bob Temple)
Editor: Sue Green
Design and Page Production: The Design Lab

Printed in the United States of America

10 9 8 7 6 5 4 3 2 1

To Our Readers: We have done our best to make sure all Internet addresses in this book were active and appropriate when we went to press. However, the author and the publisher have no control over and assume no liability for the material available on those Internet sites or on other Web sites they may link to. Any comments or suggestions can be sent by e-mail to comments@enslow.com or to the address on the back cover.

Photographs © 2007: AP Photo/Richard Carson: 10; AP Photo/Manuel Balce Ceneta: 101; AP Photo/Jeff Chiu: 3, 4; AP Photo/Richard Drew: 47; AP Photo/Jennifer Graylock: 28, 42, 99; AP Photo/Ann Heisenfelt: 105; AP Photo/Lawrence Jackson: 77; AP Photo/Julie Jacobson, file: 3, 75; AP Photo/Fred Jewell: 70; AP Photo/Bill Kostroun: 22, 58, 67, 72; AP Photo/Mark Lennihan: cover, 1, 81; AP Photo/Donna McWilliam: 51; AP Photo/Robert Mecea: 3, 91; AP Photo/Chris O'Meara: 83; AP Photo/Marcio Jose Sanchez: 7; AP Photo/Ariel Schalit: 93; AP Photo/Kathy Willens: 110; AP Photo/Ronen Zilberman: 19

Cover Photo: Tiki Barber carries the ball in the 2001 NFC Championship Game against the Minnesota Vikings.

CONTENTS

Tiki Barber breaks through the Oakland defense.

CHAPTER ONE

Tiki Equals Excitement

The New York Giants needed a big play, something to get their offense clicking against the Raiders at the always-hostile Network Associates Coliseum in Oakland, California. It was midway through the first quarter of their 2005 Week 17 game. The Giants' offense had netted only 10 yards on 7 plays in what some had called a meaningless game. The game was very meaningful to the Giants, however. A week earlier, they lost to the Washington Redskins and let a chance to win their first NFC East Division title since 2000 slip through their hands.

New York had a playoff spot wrapped up. It could be satisfied with that accomplishment. At the beginning of the season, few believed that feat was possible. One more win, though, and the Giants would be champions again. The Raiders were not going to the playoffs, and all they could hope to do was play the role of spoiler.

The beginning of the game had not gone as the Giants had planned. But one particular plan had served the team well all season: Give the ball to Tiki Barber. Barber, one of the game's most electrifying players, had come through for the Giants time and time again. They needed him to do it one more time.

On the Giants' eighth play, after a penalty had pushed the team back to its own 5-yard line, Barber provided the spark the team sought. He took a handoff up the middle, eluded a linebacker, and cut to the outside. On the way, wide receiver Plaxico Burress made a key block of a defensive back. Now it was a foot race, and Barber rarely loses such contests. As he sped down the field, Barber may have been thinking of all the childhood races he ran against

TIKI BARBER FILE
Height: 5' 10"
Weight: 200 pounds
Date of birth: April 7, 1975
Position: Running back
College: University of Virginia
NFL team: New York Giants
Acquired: Second-round draft pick, 1997
Hometown: Roanoke, Virginia

Barber runs downfield against the Oakland Raiders December 31, 2005.

his twin brother, Ronde, who plays defensive back for the Tampa Bay Buccaneers.

The Oakland crowd let out a collective groan as Barber skirted past the last Raiders defenders and finished an amazing 95-yard touchdown run. It was the longest run in franchise history. The previous record of 91 yards, set by Hap Moran against the Green Bay Packers in 1930, had stood for 75 years. The touchdown also made Barber the team's all-time rushing touchdown leader with 50, breaking a tie with former Giant Rodney Hampton.

The Raiders did not roll over, though. Oakland's Kerry Collins, who was the Giants' quarterback during their 2000 Super Bowl season, threw 3 touchdowns. His last—a 44-yard scoring pass to Randy Moss—pulled Oakland to within six points late in the third quarter.

On the next possession, Barber carried twice for 10 yards. A key pass from Giants quarterback Eli Manning to Burress for 17 yards helped set up a 46-yard field goal by Jay Feely. It was the kicker's third field goal in the game and increased the New York lead to 30–21.

Giants fans received a real scare the next time New York gained possession. An Oakland defender rolled onto Barber's ankle after he made a short reception. As ESPN went to a commercial, Barber lay on the ground, writhing in pain. But he was back up shortly and was able to jog to the sidelines.

Oakland threatened late in the fourth quarter by advancing all the way to the Giants' one-yard line. But the Giants' defense stuffed three consecutive handoffs to fullback Zack Crockett. On fourth down, Collins tried to sneak it in but was met by a wall of defenders. The Giants had held.

Barber helped the team close out the win with a 9-yard carry that went for a first down. The team ran out the clock and secured a 30–21 win. The win improved the Giants' record to 11–5 and, most important, earned them the division championship. The victory also guaranteed Ronde Barber's Buccaneers a playoff spot.

The division championship marked the Giants' twenty-first—the most by any team in the league. But this one meant a little more. During a three-week span earlier in the season, the team lost both of its owners, Wellington Mara and Bob Tisch, to cancer.

THE GIANTS' BIRTHDAY

The New York Giants played their first game on October 11, 1925, against the Frankford Yellow Jackets. The Giants finished 8–4 in their inaugural season, winning 7 of their 9 home games. The late Tim Mara purchased the team in 1925 for $500.

"To be able to give this title to the Mara and Tisch families, to be the team of record for their deaths is something that's special for a lot of us, especially those who knew those two men and their families," Barber said after the game.[1]

INTO THE RECORD BOOKS

The long scoring run against Oakland served as the topper to a season filled with highlights for Barber. He finished the victory with 203 rushing yards on 28 carries and caught 6 passes for another 60 yards. His

Barber runs down the sideline for a gain of 70 yards against the Houston Texans.

263 yards from scrimmage (rushing yards plus receiving yards) was the third highest in franchise history. Barber already held the No. 1 spot with 276 yards against the Philadelphia Eagles in 2002.

Running for such incredible yardage had become commonplace for Barber in 2005. His 203-yard performance in Oakland marked the third time he topped the 200-yard mark that season. In fact, in the team's previous eighty years of existence, Giants runners had run for 200 yards or more in a game only three times.

Barber plays much bigger than his five-foot ten-inch, 200-pound frame. He is often classified as a "slasher" type of back, one who darts and dances through defenses rather than powering through tacklers. It is true that Barber's quick feet and elusiveness make him well-equipped to catch passes out of the backfield and make moves to the outside. However, he is not one to shy away from ramming the ball up the middle where 300-pound defensive tackles and 250-pound linebackers roam.

NEW YORK, NEW YORK

New York is the third largest state in America in population (more than 19 million, estimated) after California and Texas, according to the U.S. Census Bureau's 2005 statistics. New York City is the largest city in the country with a population greater than 8 million. The New York City metro area, which includes people living in the immediate surrounding area, is the world's fifth largest with more than 16 million. The largest metro area in the world is Tokyo, Japan, with more than 28 million people.

In fact, many of Barber's big plays—such as the long touchdown run against Oakland—begin in the middle of the field before he uses his vision and shiftiness to race to the outside. It took a while for Barber to earn the respect of the league as a complete running back and shed the label of being too small, especially playing in New York, where the media treats athletes like celebrities. But Barber knew what he could do if given the chance. And in 2005, he was better than ever.

BETTER WITH AGE

Barber made his first Pro Bowl appearance in 2004, but critics wondered if he had truly risen to the ranks of the game's elite runners. Perhaps he would crash back to earth in 2005. Conventional wisdom in the NFL says running backs begin to decline when they reach thirty years of age. Barber turned thirty after the 2004 season. Barber's critics soon learned, however, that this little Giant was just taking flight.

He finished 2005 with 1,860 rushing yards, easily passing his own franchise record of 1,518 yards set a year earlier and giving him 8,787 career rushing yards. Only twelve other players in league history had run for 1,800 yards in a season. He also pulled in 54 receptions for 530 yards, giving him another franchise record: 2,390 total yards. It was the most yards ever gained by a player over thirty years old and the second most in league history. Only Marshall Faulk had recorded more. In 1999, Faulk earned 2,429 yards for the St. Louis Rams.

ELITE COMPANY

When it comes to piling up yards from scrimmage, few do it better than Tiki Barber. His incredible 2005 season landed him on a list with some of the NFL's all-time greats. Here are the top five yards-from-scrimmage seasons in league history:

RANK	YARDS	PLAYER
1	2,429	Marshall Faulk, St. Louis Rams, 1999
2	2,390	Tiki Barber, New York Giants, 2005
3	2,370	LaDainian Tomlinson, San Diego Chargers, 2003
4	2,358	Barry Sanders, Detroit Lions, 1997
5	2,314	Marcus Allen, Los Angeles Raiders, 1985

For the second straight season, Barber led the league in total yards and made the Pro Bowl. For the first time, however, he was named to the All-Pro team. He finished fourth in voting for the MVP award.

Barber set another record in 2005 for which he can be especially proud. One of the reasons Barber was drafted in the second round rather than the first in 1997 was his lack of size. Many NFL scouts believed he did not have the muscle and bulk to withstand the constant pounding running backs absorb. But the Giants kept feeding Barber the ball in 2005. He carried 357 times, passing the team mark of 341 set by Joe Morris in 1986.

In fact, Barber proved over a five-year stretch from 2002–06 to be one of the NFL's most durable backs. During that span, he played in all 80 of the Giants' games and led the team in rushing every game. Equally impressive as a receiver, Barber finished the 2006 season first on the team's all-time receptions list with 586.

"I've always believed if you work hard, harder than the next guy, you'll get farther than you ever thought you would," said Barber, who praises his teammates for their part in his successes.[2]

MAGICAL SEASON COMES TO AN END

The week after the victory in Oakland, the Giants hosted the Carolina Panthers in the NFC Wildcard Playoffs. In a disappointing end to a season in which so much went so right, everything went wrong against Carolina. New York gained only 132 yards and ran just half the amount of offensive plays the Panthers did (71–35). In the end, the Panthers won easily, 23–0.

The loss was especially disappointing for Barber. He managed only 41 yards rushing for the day. Shortly after the game he said, "They attacked our schemes. They attacked our tendencies and it was frustrating."[3]

"I've always believed if you work hard, harder than the next guy, you'll get farther than you ever thought you would."

—Tiki Barber

It was a difficult weekend for the Barber family. The day before the Giants were eliminated, Ronde's Buccaneers were defeated by the Washington Redskins 17–10. Ronde flew to New York and watched from the sidelines as his brother's team played. The Barber brothers are always there for each other.

Neither the Giants nor the Buccaneers had played up to their capabilities, and both teams were forced to look to the future. Unlike playoff series in professional baseball, basketball, and hockey, one slipup in the NFL playoffs and a season is lost.

"I believe we still have a lot to be proud of," Barber said.[4]

CHAPTER TWO

Brothers and Best Friends

The Barber twins were born on April 7, 1975. Ronde is the older twin, by a whole seven minutes. They entered the world earlier than their parents, James and Geraldine Barber, expected. Since the twin babies were born prematurely, they were smaller than normal. Each had to be placed in an incubator, a medical device that helps babies develop.

While the twins were in the incubators, the answer to one of the questions Tiki is often asked—How did you get your name?—could be found.

At Virginia Tech—where James starred as a running back—Tiki's parents had a friend who was an exchange student from Zaire. When he saw how Tiki was tossing and turning in the incubator, he suggested the name Atiim Kiambu. The Swahili term translates to "fiery-tempered king." Ronde's birth name is Jamael Oronde, which means "first-born son."

The name Tiki is a shortened version of his given name, taking the "ti" from Atiim and the "ki" from Kiambu. Tiki later said he was happy to be given the nickname because it rolled off the tongue more easily and won him a lot of young fans when he became an NFL player.

James played football in the short-lived World Football League. Beyond that, the twins do not know much about him. He left the family when they were only four years old, leaving Geraldine to raise her sons as a single mother. Tiki and Ronde have had little contact with their father. Tiki said he has never talked to his father about why he left.

WHERE'S ZAIRE?

Located in central Africa, Zaire existed from 1971 to 1997. The area is now known as the Democratic Republic of the Congo. A portion of the Congo is still often referred to as Zaire.

A LEAGUE OF THEIR OWN

The World Football League was a professional football league, separate from the NFL, that played in 1974 and part of 1975. While the league didn't last long, it produced some notable NFL coaches, such as Marty Schottenheimer, Jack Pardee, and Lindy Infante. John McVay, who coached the WFL team in Memphis, served as the New York Giants' coach from 1976 to 1978.

"There is a little bit of animosity on my part and understanding, as I got older, how hard it was for my mother," said Tiki. "Eventually, I think I'll find a way to deal with it and become a part of his life."[1]

Geraldine had to fill all the parenting roles and find a way to provide for her boys. She did so by working two jobs, sometimes three. Twelve-hour workdays were normal for her.

Geraldine was a strong woman, however. She had known pain as a child herself. Her father, a military man, died in the Vietnam War in 1967 before her fifteenth birthday. She was determined to provide Tiki and Ronde with everything they would need to become successful adults.

THE VIETNAM WAR

The Vietnam War was a conflict between North Vietnam and South Vietnam. The United States, an ally of South Vietnam, was involved from 1965 until 1973. On April 30, 1975, the war ended with the North's victory over the South.

"We had no worries," said Ronde. "We didn't have a lot of money, but we didn't struggle. My mom always provided for us."[2]

The Barbers, who are African American, grew up in a predominately white neighborhood in Roanoke, Virginia. Tiki and Ronde were rather small boys. Those two factors made them different from many of their friends, and both were a little shy early on in their lives. In fact, they often would not talk to people they did not know. But they always had each other.

Tiki (right) poses with his twin brother, Ronde, after practice for the Pro Bowl in Hawaii February 9, 2005.

"I have distinct memories of going to bed and knowing my mother was leaving (for work) and just crying in bed," said Tiki. "I was so thankful that I had a twin brother who was always there for me. We supported each other through tough times in our lives."[3]

COMING INTO THEIR OWN

One way Geraldine helped her sons overcome their shyness was to encourage them to participate in sports. Through sports, Tiki and Ronde learned the importance of teamwork and communication. And it just so happened that they were both gifted athletes. While they might not have been as big as some of their peers, they were both fast runners and quick learners. They played a variety of sports and excelled at just about everything they tried.

Their mother had a steadfast rule: no practice until all the homework was done. She also made sure that they played on the same teams. She wanted them to be together, but it was also practical. She had to juggle driving them back and forth to practices with her work schedule. Together, they made it all work, and Geraldine found a way to attend nearly every game.

Besides Geraldine, few could tell the Barber twins apart. In fact, their mother even made a habit of writing each boy's name on the bottom of his shoes so

AGAINST ALL ODDS

In 1977, as two-year olds, Tiki and Ronde experienced a type of seizure known as febrile seizures, common in premature babies. It's not typical for twins to have seizures at the same time, but Tiki and Ronde did until they were five years old. Doctors told their mother that they would never be able to play contact sports. Tiki and Ronde, obviously, had other ideas.

their babysitters could tell the boys apart. The Barber boys had become inseparable and formed a special bond in childhood that lasts to this day.

Like all siblings, Tiki and Ronde had their share of quarrels, but they never lost sight of their love for each other. Their mother stressed family above all else, and that led Tiki and Ronde to have a relationship built on the positive aspects of life. They competed against each other, but rather than trying to outdo the other twin, they used the other's accomplishments as goals.

Still, the Barbers' zeal to push one another occasionally yielded unexpected results. One such episode that taught them a valuable life lesson stayed so fresh in their minds that they eventually used it as the storyline to a children's book they co-authored in 2004 titled *By My Brother's Side*.

The book is an account of a summertime accident Tiki suffered as he tried to impress his brother with a bicycle stunt. Tiki's knee was badly injured in the crash and required more than thirty stitches. As he recovered, he was forced to sit out the baseball season and miss out on all the fun Ronde was having.

The story reveals how Ronde helped Tiki cope with the situation by keeping his brother mentally involved and being a positive influence during his recovery.

"He was the first person right by my side," said Tiki. "It's a figurative term—the title of the book— but he literally was right by my side. I was laid up for

Ronde (right) visits Tiki at Giants Stadium January 5, 2001, as the Giants prepare for the Eastern Conference Championship game.

a long time. (Ronde) made sure that I was aware of what was going on. In the book he says, 'I'll hit a home run for you. I'll play for both of us today.' He would do things like that. That made me feel less like I wasn't involved."[4]

Later in the book, Tiki attends one of Ronde's baseball games with his mother and wonders aloud if he will ever be able to run fast again. She urges him to believe in himself. Geraldine always inspired her sons to strive for excellence.

The story concludes with a healed Tiki joining Ronde on the Pee-Wee football field and the boys promising each other that they will chase their dreams together.

DREAM CHASERS

As Tiki and Ronde grew and became more [...] with organized sports, their athletic roles became more defined. They were excellent track stars and fantastic football players. In football, Tiki played on the offensive side of the ball while Ronde played on the defense. Whether by design or not, the Barber brothers played different positions in every sport and never once competed for a spot against each other. In fact, in junior high school Ronde even went on a diet so he and Tiki could wrestle in different weight classes.

Regardless of the sport, Tiki and Ronde always rooted for each other to succeed. And with each individual triumph, the other worked even harder to match it.

"We competed against each other in a way that's like, OK, I want you to be successful but at the same time I want to be successful at whatever I'm doing," said Tiki.[5]

While their mother always made sure the boys played on the same teams, she also made

SEEING DOUBLE

According to the National Center for Health Statistics, 3.1 percent of all births are twins. Ten sets of twins have played in the NFL. Twin offensive linemen Paul and Pat McQuistan were both drafted in 2006 and will become the eleventh set. Paul was drafted by the Oakland Raiders, Pat by the Dallas Cowboys. Tiki's teammate Michael Strahan is the father of twin daughters.

sure they were in different classes in school. They even went to different kindergartens. She was setting the groundwork for them to develop as individuals.

By the time Tiki and Ronde reached high school, they had become two of the best athletes in the whole area. They played football and ran track and excelled at both. The biggest news in town was the talented twi•.s at Cave Spring High.

FAMOUS BARBERS

Tiki and Ronde Barber were inducted into the Virginia High School Hall of Fame in October of 2006. Some other notable members of the hall include NBA greats Moses Malone, Ralph Sampson, and Grant Hill.

In track, Ronde was a hurdler while Tiki competed in the jumping events. Ronde was the Virginia state champion in the 55-meter hurdles every year except when he was a freshman. He won the national championship as a senior with a time of 7.19 seconds. Tiki, meanwhile, won the state long jump title as a junior and senior. As a junior, he ranked third nationally in the event. He added a state triple jump title as a senior. Together, the Barbers combined for eight individual state championships in indoor and outdoor track and hold eleven school records.

Despite their success on the track, the Barbers were actually better football players. Tiki played running back and ran for 3,608 career yards in high school. Ronde set a school record with 11 interceptions in one season. Tiki got a taste of what Ronde's athletic life was like during his senior year. For a couple of games, Tiki filled in at safety for Ronde, who had suffered a collarbone injury. The switch showed Tiki's versatility, but everyone knew his future was as a runner.

It can be easy for a young athlete to let success go to his head, but Geraldine would not allow it. Homework always came first in the Barber household, and it paid off. Ronde graduated from Cave Spring with a 3.3 grade-point average (GPA). Tiki was the class of 1993's valedictorian with a perfect 4.0 GPA.

When graduation finally came, Tiki and Ronde faced a big decision: Where would they go to college? With their strong grades and athletic ability, nearly every college in the country wanted them. They kept their options open, but the one thing they knew for sure was wherever they ended up, they would end up there together.

Making the Grade

Deciding which college to attend was a difficult choice for Tiki and Ronde. It was the biggest decision they had faced in their young lives. Whatever their choice, they were going to have to leave their mother for the first time. A new life awaited them, but the next step to manhood was one they would take together.

"It was a natural that we would not go separate ways after high school," said Ronde. "We knew without ever sitting down and talking about it that we were going to the same school, and most of the coaches recruited us that way."[1]

The Barbers narrowed their choice to Michigan, Penn State, Clemson, and Virginia. A snowstorm forced them to miss the Michigan trip. They figured that meant they were not supposed to go there. They also did not make the trip to Penn State, but they visited Clemson and Virginia and narrowed it down to one of the two.

Their mother hoped they would choose Virginia Tech, her alma mater, because she was familiar with the school. It also was closer to their home. That would have made it easier for her to attend their games. In the end, though, the Barbers decided the University of Virginia was the school for them.

STARTING OVER

Tiki and Ronde were no longer the big men on campus as they had been at Cave Spring High. Their college teammates were gifted athletes, and the Barbers would have to prove themselves all over again. They also had to adjust to a new lifestyle. They had to take care of themselves. Mom would not be around to make snacks or do the laundry.

"I had no idea when to add fabric softener or what kind of detergent to use or anything," Tiki said with a laugh.[2]

Not long after they enrolled in college, Tiki and Ronde found they had yet another challenge, but they

BRAINS AND BRAWN
Tiki Barber was a fantastic student. In fact, he attended the University of Virginia on an academic, not athletic, scholarship.

Ronde (left) and Tiki attend a cancer benefit in New York.

were eager to meet this one. With the boys out of the house, Geraldine decided to pursue one of her own goals and went back to school to earn her master's degree. Tiki said, "Literally every week, she would call and tell us 'I'm making straight A's. What are you guys doing?' We competed against Mom all the way through college."[3]

The competition on the football field was as strong as their mother's report cards. Coach George Welsh knew both Tiki and Ronde had the potential to be great players, but it would take time for them to develop. He was thrilled when they signed with Virginia but said, "We are not expecting miracles."[4]

It was a good thing their coach was not expecting miracles, because success did not come quickly at Virginia for either Tiki or Ronde. In fact, Ronde was redshirted his freshman year, and Tiki only carried the ball 16 times for 45 yards the whole season as the Cavaliers went 7–5.

"We were not expecting miracles."

—George Welsh

The next season, both Barbers were on the field, but it was Ronde who made the most impact. After sitting out his first year of college, Ronde won a starting cornerback position. He became a star in his very first game. He made 15 tackles and intercepted a pass in a 41–17 loss to Florida State, which was ranked No. 3 in the nation at the time. Ronde was named the Chevrolet Player of the Game by ABC Sports, and Tiki got his first taste of what it was like to be the lesser known brother.

Tiki got into the game late and played well. He topped 100 yards rushing for the first time as a Cavalier (108 yards on 12 carries), but it was not a sign of things to come. He played the rest of the year sparingly as a reserve tailback, while Kevin Brooks led the team with 741 rushing yards.

Meanwhile, Ronde enjoyed a sensational season. He finished second in the nation in interceptions with 8 and was named to the third-team All-America squad. He also became the first Virginia freshman to earn All-Atlantic Coast Conference (ACC) honors. The team finished with a 9–3 record, tied for third place in the ACC, and capped its season with a 20–10 win against

> **"Ronde kept telling me that Coach Welsh was just trying to make me a better player, and now I can see that."**
>
> **—Tiki Barber**

Texas Christian in the Independence Bowl. Tiki used his brother's success as extra motivation to better himself. Tiki spent long hours in the weight room to add muscle.

It was difficult for Tiki to handle being just another member of the team rather than the star. His coach kept on him, pushing him to work harder. Like their childhood when Tiki was forced to sit out the baseball season with an injured knee, Ronde kept his brother's spirits up.

"Ronde kept telling me that Coach Welsh was just trying to make me a better player, and now I can see that," said Tiki.[5]

BREAKOUT SEASON

Tiki worked hard after his sophomore season. His effort paid off. He was named the team's starting running back heading into the 1995 campaign. Ronde was already established as one of the team's best players, but he was not completely healthy coming into the season. He had undergone surgery on his left foot after the 1994 season and twisted his right ankle during preseason. But expectations for the Barbers and the team were high. Virginia entered the season ranked No. 17 in the country.

The very first game, the Pigskin Classic, presented a stiff challenge. The Cavaliers faced Michigan, ranked No. 14 in the country, at the "Big House" in Ann Arbor, Michigan. The Wolverines' stadium is known as the "Big House" because it is the largest college football stadium in the nation. Its seating capacity is 107,501. The Michigan crowd can get very loud and always makes it tough on opposing teams.

THE BIG HOUSE GETS BIGGER

Michigan Stadium opened in 1927 with the ability to seat 72,000 fans. It has experienced several renovations through the years. In May of 2006, plans were unveiled for more renovations to improve concessions, widen seats and aisles, create a new press box, and add restrooms. When the renovations are complete, the seating capacity will exceed 108,000.

The Michigan fans were stunned, however, as the Cavaliers came out firing. After quarterback Mike Groh ran for a one-yard score, Tiki silenced the crowd with an incredible 81-yard touchdown run. It was the second longest touchdown run in school history.

The Wolverines, however, were not ranked so highly for nothing. They gamely fought back from a 17–0 deficit and pulled to within five points on a 31-yard touchdown pass from quarterback Scott Dreisbach to Mercury Hayes in the fourth quarter.

With 2:35 showing on the clock, Michigan got the ball back on its own 20-yard line with one last chance for the winning score. Dreisbach moved the team to the Virginia 15 with only 12 seconds left. Three straight incomplete passes left time for only one play.

Dreisbach dropped back to pass and looked Hayes' way. Ronde was in coverage, but Hayes had slipped by him. Dreisbach threw high. Ronde could not reach it. Hayes made the catch and desperately tried to drag his foot inbounds along the back right side of the end zone. Was he in? Did it count? The referee took a hard look and threw his arms up in the air—touchdown Michigan. The final score was Michigan 18, Virginia 17.

It was a devastating loss for the Cavaliers and the Barbers. Tiki had cemented the running back position with 113 rushing yards, gaining an average of more than 9 yards each time he carried the ball, but seeing his brother beaten for the winning score was tough to stomach. Yet Ronde stayed upbeat. The season was young, and the Barbers were ready to shine.

The Cavaliers rebounded with five straight wins. Tiki ran for more than 100 yards in three of the wins, highlighted by a 119-yard, 4-touchdown game against Georgia Tech. The team then lost two of its next three, falling to North Carolina and No. 16 Texas. The loss to the Longhorns, like the loss to Michigan, was a stinging one-point defeat. Next up was the team's toughest test yet: the big, bad Seminoles from Florida State.

PRIME-TIME PERFORMANCE

Florida State was ranked No. 2 in the country and sported a 7–0 record. The Seminoles came to Scott Stadium in Charlottesville, Virginia, for a Thursday night game on ESPN that the whole nation would see. Few gave the Cavaliers much chance to win. After all, Florida State had won all 29 of its conference games since joining the ACC in 1992 and had scored 40 or more points in every game that season. In three of their games, the Seminoles had scored more than 70 points. But Welsh knew his players—especially his star running back—could match up with the Seminoles.

"(Tiki) went from being a good outside runner to being a big-league tailback," Welsh said before the game. "He is pretty clever and I am not sure I have ever coached a running back quite like him before."[6]

Florida State had never seen a runner quite like Barber, either. He ran over the Seminoles,

GREAT PLAYERS IN GREAT GAMES
Tiki and Ronde Barber played in two of the most memorable college football games ever. Collegefootballnews.com rated Virginia's 18–17 season-opening loss to Michigan in 1995 as the No. 51 greatest college football ending. The Cavaliers' 33–28 win against Florida State in 1995 ranked as the No. 87 greatest game ever played.

dashed around them, and had them on their heels throughout the game as the Cavaliers built a 33–21 lead in the first Thursday-night college football game played in Charlottesville.

Like the Michigan game that opened the season, Virginia would have to battle to the very end as the Seminoles mounted a comeback. With a little more than 6 minutes remaining to play, Florida State's Warrick Dunn ran for a 7-yard touchdown to trim the Virginia lead to 33–28. The Seminoles got the ball back at their own 20 with 1:37 left to play, a situation eerily similar to the season opener at Ann Arbor.

Florida State quarterback Danny Kanell moved the offense to the Virginia 6 with time left for one more play. Rather than passing, the Seminoles

YOU CAN ALWAYS GO HOME

Anthony Poindexter was a freshman in 1995 when he helped make the game-saving tackle of Florida State's Warrick Dunn in Virginia's thrilling 33–28 victory against the No. 2 Seminoles. He went on to have an outstanding college career, earning All-ACC recognition three times and winning the 1998 ACC Defensive Player of the Year award. His senior season ended in the seventh game when he suffered a knee injury that required reconstructive surgery. The Baltimore Ravens used a seventh-round pick to draft Poindexter in 1999. He spent two seasons with the Ravens before ending his NFL career with the Cleveland Browns. He is now a member of the Virginia coaching staff, guiding the team's running backs.

> **"I was just thinking to myself, 'No touchdown.' I was expecting a pass, everyone was. But the ball was snapped directly to Dunn, and from there my instincts took over."**
>
> **—Adrian Burnim**

surprised the Cavaliers with a direct snap to Dunn, who weaved his way through traffic up the middle toward the goal line. Dunn reached out as far as he could as he was met by safeties Anthony Poindexter and Adrian Burnim. A host of Virginia defenders piled on, and no one was really sure if Dunn had crossed the goal line.

"I was just thinking to myself, 'No touchdown,'" Burnim said. "I was expecting a pass, everyone was. But the ball was snapped directly to Dunn, and from there my instincts took over."[7]

The referee rushed in to make the call. Would he extend his hands, signaling touchdown and another bitter defeat? The officials pulled players from the pile. The referee emphatically signaled that Dunn was down.

He did not make it. The defense had held. Fans stormed the field as the unthinkable had really happened.

Virginia had beaten the shocked Seminoles, and Tiki had played a starring role. His early 69-yard scoring run answered Florida State's first score, and when it was all over, Tiki had amassed 311 all-purpose yards, the second highest total in school history at the time. He ran for 193 yards, received for 45 more, and added another 73 on punt returns. He was the talk of college football. Talk of Tiki as a Heisman Trophy candidate was also beginning.

The Cavaliers were national news. They continued their winning ways with a 31–18 victory against Maryland behind 116 rushing yards from Tiki. A loss to Virginia Tech the next week left the team at 8–4 heading into the Peach Bowl against Georgia in Atlanta.

The Peach Bowl had a wild finish, mirroring Virginia's drama-filled season. It looked as if the Bulldogs had escaped certain defeat when they returned a fumble for a touchdown in the closing minutes. However, Virginia's Demetrius "Pete" Allen returned the ensuing kickoff 83 yards for a touchdown with less than a minute to play for a breathtaking 34–27 victory.

Tiki had another fine game. He rushed for 103 yards and a touchdown and was named his team's most outstanding offensive player. It was a gratifying end to a special season. Tiki was named a third-team All-American and was one of eight finalists for the

YES, THAT WAS HINES PLAYING QB

Pittsburgh Steelers wide receiver Hines Ward played quarterback for Georgia against Virginia in the 1995 Peach Bowl. Ward was named his team's most valuable offensive player as he set school bowl records for passing attempts, yards, completions, and total offense. He completed 31 of 59 passes for 413 yards and ran 9 times for 56 yards for a total of 469 yards. He was drafted by the Steelers in 1998 and converted into a wide receiver. Ward has become one of the NFL's top receivers and was named a Super Bowl MVP. He caught 5 passes for 123 yards and a touchdown in the Steelers' 21–10 victory against the Seattle Seahawks.

Doak Walker Award, an honor given to the nation's best running back. The Cavaliers finished 9–4 and as co-champions of the ACC.

Tiki set school records in rushing yards with 1,397 and all-purpose yards with 1,906. He had run for 100 yards or more in 9 games. He was doing equally well in the classroom, earning a spot on the first-team GTE Academic All-America team.

Tiki could hardly wait for his senior season.

CHAPTER FOUR

Playing With Pride and Purpose

Life couldn't be better for Tiki Barber as he entered his senior season in 1996. He had it all. He was a team captain and starting running back for a powerful college football team. His brother, Ronde, was a starting cornerback. Tiki was making outstanding grades in the classroom. He had met the girl who would eventually become his wife, and some people in Charlottesville believed he could even win the Heisman Trophy.

Virginia entered the season ranked No. 23 in the nation, and fans had purchased a record number of season tickets. It seemed everybody wanted to watch the Virginia Cavaliers.

In some respects, Tiki did have it all. But he entered the season fearing he might lose something that meant more to him and his brother than anything in the world—their mother.

Geraldine was diagnosed with breast cancer before Tiki's senior season. She had always put her sons before herself, and, even when facing a potentially deadly disease, she still did.

"My first thought was, 'How can I screw up my kids' last year in college?'" she said.[1]

Virginia was scheduled to open the season at home against Central Michigan. Tiki and Ronde prepared for the game, but their minds were on their mother. Meanwhile, her mind was with them. She required more than nine hours of surgery to remove the cancer-filled area. The procedure is generally considered safe, but every surgery carries a certain amount of risk.

Geraldine postponed her surgery because it fell

WHAT'S IN A NAME?

Nationally, the University of Virginia athletic teams are referred to as Cavaliers, but the students often refer to the teams and players as "Wahoos" or "Hoos." How those nicknames originated is unknown. A song called "The Cavalier Song" was written in 1923 for a contest to choose an official fight song. The song won the contest but did not become a part of Virginia's tradition. It did, however, inspire the nickname "Cavaliers."

on the same day as Virginia's first game. She did not want to miss the game, so she moved the surgery to two days later.

"I've made up my mind that I'm going to survive this."

—Geraldine Barber

"Being the strong person that she is and always has been, she said, 'I don't want you guys to worry about me. I'm going to beat this. I've made up my mind that I'm going to survive this,'" recalled Tiki.[2]

With heavy hearts—and their mother in the stands—Tiki and Ronde played against Central Michigan. Tiki put on a show. The first two times he carried the ball, he went all the way for touchdowns. The Cavaliers cruised to an easy 55–21 victory, and Tiki only played one series in the second half. He finished the game with 14 carries for 147 yards.

Two days later, Geraldine had the surgery, which was successful. Though Tiki and Ronde wanted to be by her side, she instructed them not to come to the hospital during the surgery because she wanted to be awake when they saw her. Instead, she had a friend call them when it was all done. While the surgery went as the doctors had hoped, Geraldine was far from out of the woods. She faced six months of chemotherapy. She refused to let it affect her life more than it had to, though, and did not miss a single Virginia football game.

"They knew when I was scheduled for treatments," she said, "and they would call me sometimes and be comforting and touchy-feely, or at other times they would be like coaches and tell me to get off my butt and stop feeling sorry for myself."[3]

Whenever times got tough for Tiki and Ronde during the 1996 season, all they had to do was think about what their mother was going through and feed off her courage.

"She attacked (the cancer). She learned about it," said Tiki. "I think a lot of the traits that she has have made us successful in our careers."[4]

Another area of Tiki's life was also developing. He met Ginny, who became his girlfriend. Tiki had Ronde to thank for that. Ronde had wanted to go out with one of Ginny's friends, but she would not go unless Ginny went, too. So, Tiki tagged along. In time, Tiki and Ginny fell in love. They were married in May of 1999.

GOING TO THE CHAPEL OF LOVE

Tiki Barber and Ginny (Virginia) Cha were married in Charlottesville at the University Chapel in 1999 and are now the parents of two sons, Atiim Kiambu Jr. (A.J.) and Chason Cole. When they first met, Ginny had a hard time telling Tiki and Ronde apart but was able to do so by their earrings. Tiki had a hoop earring; Ronde wore a stud.

Barber and his wife, Ginny

FLYING HIGH IN 1996

The Cavaliers got off to a fast start in 1996, winning three straight after the Central Michigan game. Tiki ran for more than 100 yards in every game, including a 121-yard, 3-touchdown effort in a 37–13 victory against No. 13 Texas. The victory against the Longhorns vaulted Virginia all the way up to No. 12 in the country.

Tiki learned a valuable lesson the next week, however, when the Cavaliers traveled to Atlanta to take on Georgia Tech. During an interview, Tiki did not guarantee a victory, but the newspapers sure made it sound like he did when he told them he felt Virginia had the better players, coaches, and game plan.

The Yellow Jackets used those comments as extra motivation. They did not exactly stop Tiki, who ran for 123 yards and a touchdown, but they did pull the upset. A disheartening 13–7 loss dropped the

FAST TRACK TO SUCCESS

In addition to excelling at football, Tiki and Ronde Barber found similar success on the Virginia track team. In fact, Tiki tied the school record in the long jump (24-feet 6-inches) on his very first attempt as a freshman in 1993. Tiki earned three varsity letters on the track team. He placed second in the long jump at the IC4A Indoor Championships and seventh at the 1994 ACC Outdoor Championships. He and Ronde were part of the 4x100-meter relay team that finished fifth at the 1995 ACC Outdoor Championships.

Cavaliers all the way to No. 20 in the rankings. They had two weeks to stew over it before their next game. Tiki learned to be careful what he said. He realized his comments might not be reported the way he intended. He also learned to be humble.

Virginia rebounded with a strong 62–14 drubbing of North Carolina State. The showdown of the season loomed as the Cavaliers were set to travel to Tallahassee, Florida, to take on the No. 3 Florida State Seminoles.

Like the year before, Florida State entered the game undefeated. The Seminoles' defense keyed on Tiki, who was leading the ACC with an average of 126.3 rushing yards per game. Tiki had another big game, rushing 21 times for 150 yards and a touchdown, but Florida State was too much for the Cavaliers. The Seminoles came away with a 31–24 victory. Any chance of another conference title was pretty much gone for Virginia, but there was still plenty of football to be played.

The next week, Tiki ran for 128 yards and 2 touchdowns against Duke in a 27–3 victory. That made eight straight 100-yard games for Tiki—a new school record.

The Cavaliers could not get on a roll, however, and lost the following week to Clemson. Things did not look good heading into a showdown with No. 6 North Carolina. It was the final game at Scott

SPEAKING FROM EXPERIENCE

Tiki Barber was invited to give the valedictory address to the University of Virginia's graduating class of 2004. It was a special honor because, at Virginia, the students select who will give the address. Tiki inspired the audience with a thoughtful speech and urged the seniors to face the challenges in front of them. "We live in a world where there are challenges in everything that we do, but it's your opportunity to make a difference," he told the seniors. "My advice to all of you is to follow your passions and hold onto it with everything you've got."

Stadium for the seniors, but they went out in style, scoring a 20–17 upset.

The last game of the regular season was a trip to No. 17 Virginia Tech. Tiki needed 122 rushing yards to become Virginia's all-time leading rusher. He had certainly come a long way from the freshman who could barely get any playing time.

In the end, it was a bittersweet game for Tiki. He gained the yards he needed. He rushed for 162 yards, which pushed him past former Cavalier Terry Kirby into first place on the school rushing list with 3,389 career yards. But it was the Virginia Tech Hokies who came out on top with a 26–9 victory.

The loss dropped Virginia to 7–4 overall and 5–3 in conference play. The Cavaliers finished fourth in the conference. They earned a trip to the Carquest Bowl to take on No. 19 Miami (Florida), but Tiki suffered an injury early in the game and could only watch as the Hurricanes posted a 31–21 victory.

TIKI BARBER'S COLLEGE CAREER STATS

VIRGINIA CAREER RUSHING LEADERS

PLAYER	CARRIES	YARDS	TOUCHDOWNS
1. Thomas Jones 1996–99	809	3,998	36
2. Tiki Barber 1993–96	651	3,389	31
3. Terry Kirby 1989–92	567	3,348	24
4. John Papit 1947–50	537	3,238	27
5. Tommy Vigorito 1977–80	648	2,913	15

VIRGINIA CAREER ALL-PURPOSE YARDS LEADERS

PLAYER	RUSH	REC.	PR	KOR	TOT.
1. Frank Quayle 1966–68	2,695	1,145	50	1,091	4,981
2. Tiki Barber 1993–96	3,389	602	694	184	4,869
3. Thomas Jones 1996–99	3,998	571	82	47	4,698
4. Terry Kirby 1989–92	3,348	1,022	0	267	4,637
5. John Papit 1947–50	3,238	85	7	651	3,981

VIRGINIA SEASON ALL-PURPOSE YARDS LEADERS

PLAYER	RUSH	REC.	PR	KOR	TOT.
1. Thomas Jones 1999	1,798	239	17	0	2,054
2. Tiki Barber 1995	1,397	216	272	21	1,906
3. Frank Quayle 1968	1,213	426	0	230	1,869
4. Tiki Barber 1996	1,360	258	241	0	1,859
5. Bill Dudley 1941	968	60	481	89	1,674

REC.: RECEIVING
PR: PUNT RETURNS
KOR: KICKOFF RETURNS
TOT.: TOTAL

It was not the ending to his college career that Tiki had envisioned, but he had reason to be proud. He had become the all-time leading rusher in Virginia history and was named the ACC Player of the Year and a first-team academic All-American. That spring, Tiki graduated from the University of Virginia's McIntire School of Commerce with ACC Honor Roll recognition.

Years later, when asked if he could go back and change anything about his college life, Tiki said, "I don't think I would do anything differently. I think my college experience was perfect. I met my wife there, and my life turned out great because of college."[5]

The next step for Tiki was the National Football League. It would fulfill childhood dreams for both Tiki and Ronde. But they knew, after 21 years of being together, they were likely going to have to part ways.

Barber smiles while reading the award nominations.

CHAPTER FIVE

Into the NFL

Tiki and Ronde Barber knew the next chapter in their lives would be different from anything they had faced before. They were both headed to the NFL, but the chances of them going to the same team were remote.

Like Tiki, Ronde graduated from the University of Virginia's McIntire School of Commerce. Because he was redshirted as a freshman, he had another year of eligibility and could have returned to Virginia for another football season. But he opted instead to declare for the NFL Draft.

It was only fitting that Tiki and Ronde enter the NFL together. They had done pretty much everything together. In fact, they had shared a room for eighteen years and lived together in an apartment during their last three years at Virginia.

"Getting drafted was obviously something we set as a goal and had aimed to do," said Tiki. "But it was bittersweet because we knew that this run of being together, basically forever, was going to come to an end."[1]

DRAFT DAY

April 19, 1997—the day of the NFL Draft—had finally arrived. It brought promise, tension, and a touch of fear. It also brought a lot of questions. When would Tiki and Ronde be drafted? What teams would call out their names at Madison Square Garden in New York? Could Tiki and Ronde's dreams of being drafted by the same team actually come true?

". . . [Ronde and I] knew that this run of being together, basically forever, was going to come to an end."

—Tiki Barber

GUESSING GAME

NFL teams work very hard studying college players before the draft, but they're not always right about who the best players are. While many players selected early never make it on the NFL level, some late-round picks prove to be very good players. Class of '97 member Priest Holmes, who scored a franchise-record 84 touchdowns for the Kansas City Chiefs between 2001 and 2005, wasn't even drafted. Some of the players drafted in the fifth round or later in 1997 who went on to have solid careers include center Jeff Mitchell, cornerback Al Harris, defensive lineman Grady Jackson, tight end Kris Mangum, defensive lineman Jason Ferguson, and fullback Jerald Sowell.

College players sometimes have an idea which teams are interested in them, but they can never know for sure until the cards with their names written on them are sent to the podium. Some teams say very little before the draft. Others will talk up a player they are not really interested in to mask their true intentions. It makes for a day of great suspense.

The 1997 NFL Draft was not considered one of the better ones for offensive talent. In fact, few believed there would be any future offensive Hall of Famers in this class. This class was thought to be more of a defensive class, filled with players who could sack the quarterback and intercept passes. A report in *The Sporting News* predicted as many as seventeen defensive backs would be selected in the first three rounds. That was good news for Ronde but not for Tiki.

Most NFL scouts did not peg Tiki as an every-down player. They figured his smaller size would not allow him to be a 20-carry-per-game type of running back. His open-field instincts and speed made him an ideal choice as a third-down back and kick returner.

There were a few teams that experts figured might take a running back early. Mike Ditka, who coached the famed 1985 Chicago Bears to Super Bowl victory, had taken over as coach of the New Orleans Saints. The Saints had the No. 10 pick, and many felt Ditka would want to build New Orleans' running game by taking a back.

Barber carries the ball against the Cowboys.

The Tampa Bay Buccaneers, who owned the No. 12 pick, were another team that could use a runner. There was also some talk that the Cincinnati Bengals, who had the No. 14 pick, were interested in a running back after losing Garrison Hearst to free agency. Some reports suggested they liked Tiki the most of all the available backs.

Few agreed that he was the best available, however. *The Sporting News* ranked Tiki as the sixth best running back in the draft, and the forty-fifth best player overall. Ronde was not even mentioned on the list, though eleven other cornerbacks were.

One of the great things about the NFL Draft, however, is that it does not matter what the experts say. What matters is what the teams think, and most drafts have a few surprises. The 1997 draft was no different.

No running backs had been taken when it was the Saints' turn to make a pick, but they also passed on a

CAVALIERS IN THE DRAFT

VIRGINIA CAVALIERS SELECTED IN THE FIRST THREE ROUNDS OF THE 1997 NFL DRAFT

PLAYER	POSITION	ROUND	NFL TEAM
James Farrior	LB	1	Jets
Jon Harris	DE	1	Eagles
Jamie Sharper	LB	2	Ravens
Tiki Barber	RB	2	Giants
Ronde Barber	CB	3	Buccaneers

GRADING THE GIANTS' 1997 DRAFT

SPORTS ILLUSTRATED's PETER KING GAVE TAMPA BAY THE ONLY A (AN A-) IN THE 1997 DRAFT. HE GAVE THE NEW YORK GIANTS A B. HE WROTE, "RUNNING BACK TIKI BARBER, SAFETY SAM GARNES AND THIRD QUARTERBACK MIKE CHERRY WILL ALL HAVE LONG AND PRODUCTIVE CAREERS WITH THE GIANTS."

ROUND	PLAYER	POS.	COLLEGE
1	Ike Hilliard	WR	Florida
2	Tiki Barber	RB	Virginia
3	Ryan Phillips	OLB	Idaho
3	Brad Maynard	P	Ball State
4	Pete Monty	MLB	Wisconsin
5	Sam Garnes	SS	Cincinnati
6	Mike Cherry	QB	Murray State
7	Matt Keneley	DT	Southern California

back and took guard Chris Naeole from Colorado. After Atlanta took Nebraska corner Michael Booker with the No. 11 pick, Tampa Bay was "on the clock" and in need of a runner. Antowain Smith, a powerful runner from the University of Houston, was rated as the top back, but the Buccaneers decided they wanted a smaller, sleeker back. The thing was, it was not Tiki. They took Warrick Dunn from Florida State.

The Bengals passed on a back at No. 14, and another runner was not selected until the Buffalo Bills chose Smith with the No. 23 selection. The first round ended with only two running backs chosen.

With the fourth pick in the second round, the Baltimore Ravens selected Tiki's college teammate Jamie Sharper, a linebacker. Three Cavaliers had already been chosen, and Tiki was not one of them.

But Tiki's wait was almost done. Just two picks later, with the 36th overall selection, the New York Giants submitted their card. It read: Tiki Barber.

Tiki was going to the NFL. He had been selected much higher than the experts predicted and ahead of three runners rated higher than him. The only thing that could cap the day was to hear Ronde's name called.

"Mom, I want you to quit your job tomorrow. Ronde and I will take care of you."

—Tiki Barber

Eight defensive backs were chosen in the second round after Tiki was drafted, but Ronde was not among them. The second round came to a close. The third round would be held before the end of the day. There was still a possibility Ronde would be a first-day choice. All the Barbers could do was wait and hope.

CATCHING A DREAM

Three of the first five picks in the third round were running backs. With the 65th overall pick, the Dallas Cowboys took linebacker Dexter Coakley from Appalachian State. Next up were the Buccaneers, a team that had been mentioned as having interest in Tiki.

Tampa Bay sent in its card. It read: Ronde Barber.

Now it was official. Tiki and Ronde were both going to be professional football players. As boys, they had promised each other they would chase their dreams all the way to the NFL. They made it.

Geraldine Barber was extremely proud to have both of her sons drafted into the NFL and said it was second only to hearing their names called out during graduation ceremonies at Virginia.

But, later at dinner, Geraldine was moved to tears by something Tiki said. She had worked so hard for so long to raise her sons the right way. Now, Tiki leaned over and said, "Mom, I want you to quit your job tomorrow. Ronde and I will take care of you."[2]

WHAT ALMOST WAS?

The Barbers will never know for sure, but they will always wonder what might have happened if Tampa Bay hadn't selected Ronde. The Giants were only two picks away from their third-round selection when the Buccaneers used the 66th overall pick to take Ronde.

"We think the Giants would have taken Ronde a couple of picks after Tampa took him," Tiki said. "We were hoping. We were like, 'the Giants are up in two picks,' and then he got picked."

CHAPTER SIX

The Rough Early Years

The best high school football players often find that their college teammates are just as good as they are. For the college players who make it to the NFL, the talent-level shock is even greater. Being a rookie in the NFL is like starting all over again. All the players in the NFL are good, and many of them have skills and ability most college players have never seen before.

Not only do rookies have to deal with competing against better players, they also have to adjust to living in new cities. In Tiki Barber's case, it was not just any city. It was New York City—the largest city in the whole country.

Barber visited New York for the first time during his junior year at Virginia, but this was a new beginning. Barber was eager to take on the new challenges. The first challenge was to win a spot on the team. The Giants were waiting for former No. 1 pick Tyrone Wheatley to blossom. New York used the No. 17 pick in the 1995 draft on Wheatley, who ran for 4,186 yards and 47 touchdowns at the University of Michigan. But Wheatley had yet to live up to his first-round draft status.

Wheatley had rushed for only 645 yards in his first two years and only started one game. Meanwhile, veteran Rodney Hampton, whose career was winding down, had started most of the games since 1995 and had rushed for 2,009 yards during that span.

HOME OF THE GIANTS

After playing in five different stadiums in their first fifty years, the Giants moved into Giants Stadium, located in East Rutherford, New Jersey, in 1976. New York played its first game in the stadium on October 10, 1976, against the Dallas Cowboys in front of a sellout crowd. In 1984, the New York Jets began playing in the stadium, too. Other football teams that have called Giants Stadium home include the New Jersey Generals of the United States Football League, the New York/New Jersey Knights of the World League of American Football, and the New York/New Jersey Hitmen of the XFL. Today, the stadium seats more than 80,000.

Barber carries the ball December 28, 2002, in a game against the Philadelphia Eagles.

When opening day came, however, first-year coach Jim Fassel had made his choice. His starting running back was Tiki Barber.

The first game of the season was a home game at Giants Stadium against their division rival, the Philadelphia Eagles. The Eagles had gone to the playoffs the year before with the league's fifth-rated defense. Most experts predicted New York would finish last in the division. A win against the Eagles would build momentum for the rest of the season.

Barber ran for 88 yards on 20 carries and scored a touchdown as the Giants surprised the Eagles, 31–17. He also had 32 receiving yards, giving him more than 100 yards from scrimmage for the game. The fans even chanted "Tiki, Tiki," during the game. It was a perfect way to start his career.

The Giants lost their next two games. Barber scored touchdowns in both games but was not gaining many yards. He rushed for 17 yards in a loss to the Jacksonville Jaguars and 64 in a loss to the Baltimore Ravens. New York lost its third straight game and was terrible on offense in a 13–3 loss to the St. Louis Rams. Barber gained only 4 yards on 9 rushing attempts.

It went from bad to worse the next week in a win against New Orleans. Barber suffered an injury to his right knee and had to miss the next four games. Wheatley assumed the starting job, and the team got on a roll, winning five of its next seven games with one tie.

Barber returned to the field in Week 11 but was not getting much playing time beyond special teams. He carried the ball a total of just 18 times in four games leading up to the Week 15 rematch against Philadelphia. Wheatley suffered an ankle sprain against the Eagles, and Fassel put the ball back into Barber's hands.

Eager to prove himself again, Barber had his best game of the year. He dashed through the Eagles' defenders for 114 rushing yards on 21 carries and scored a touchdown. It was the first 100-yard rushing game of his career. To make things even better, the Giants won, 31–21.

Barber kept the starting position for the rest of the year. He ran for 32 yards the next week as the Giants' defense stumped the Washington Redskins in a 30–10 victory. The Giants' defense had taken some giant strides in 1997 and led the league in takeaways.

New York only had one game left—at Dallas. The Giants were hot. They needed to play their best against quarterback Troy Aikman, running back Emmitt Smith, and the rest of the Cowboys who had made Dallas a three-time Super Bowl winner in the 1990s. And play their best they did. The Giants surged out to a 20–0 lead and limited the Cowboys to a single touchdown for a 20–7 victory. Barber led the Giants' offense with 82 rushing yards, while the defense held Dallas to only 184 total yards. In the process, the Giants became the NFC East champions.

PLAYING BIG AGAINST "BIG D"

Maybe it was seeing Dallas star Emmitt Smith on the other sideline that prompted Tiki Barber to have big games against the Cowboys. In college, Virginia coach George Welsh said, "Some of (Barber's) moves are like those that (Smith) makes."

The Giants had plenty of momentum going into their Wildcard playoff game against the visiting Minnesota Vikings. New York built a 22–10 fourth-quarter lead only to see it slip away in the final moments. With less than two minutes to play, the Vikings scored on a pass from Brad Johnson to Jake Reed. Then, the Vikings recovered an onside kick to set up a game-winning field goal.

MIRACLE AT THE MEADOWLANDS

The Minnesota Vikings' comeback victory against the New York Giants in the 1997 playoffs was a bitter pill for the fans at Giants Stadium to swallow. However, it was not the most incredible ending to a game played there. That came in 1978 in a game now known as the Miracle at the Meadowlands. The Giants held a 17-12 lead against the Philadelphia Eagles and were running out the clock. The Eagles were out of timeouts. All the Giants had to do was down the ball. Instead, New York quarterback Joe Pisarcik tried to hand off to fullback Larry Csonka. Unbelievably, the ball was fumbled, and Eagles cornerback Herman Edwards—who later became coach of the New York Jets—scooped it up and ran for the winning touchdown. Because of this play, teams today will rarely do anything but have their quarterback kneel down when they are running out the clock.

The 23–22 loss left a bitter taste in the Giants' mouths. Losing a game they seemingly had in control made for a long off-season and a lot of second-guessing by the media. Barber, who gained only 29 rushing yards in the loss, also was targeted. The questions about whether he was big enough to be a full-time player resurfaced. He finished the year with 511 rushing yards and 299 receiving yards. Fullback Charles Way led the team with 698 rushing yards, and Wheatley totaled 583. Plus, Barber missed a lot of time due to the injury, which only fueled more questions.

Despite the playoff loss, the team had accomplished more in 1997 than most thought it could, and Fassel was named the coach of the year. The future seemed very bright.

A STEP BACK

Prior to the 1998 season, the Giants signed free agent running back Gary Brown. Brown had spent his first five seasons playing for the Houston Oilers, topping 1,000 yards in 1993. In 1997, he led the San Diego Chargers with 945 yards rushing—more than Barber, Wheatley, or Way.

When the season-opening game against the Redskins rolled around, however, it was Barber in the backfield as the starter again. The Giants won 31–24, but Barber could not get on track. He gained only 37 yards rushing and was held to 32 yards the next week in a loss to Oakland. Barber continued to start the next two games but only had 4 rushing attempts. In the fifth game of the season, the Giants made a switch, naming Brown the new starter.

"It helped tremendously to have someone as close as he was to me in the same industry."

—Tiki Barber

Unlike his rookie season when Barber lost the starting job due to injury, this time he was replaced. Fortunately, he had Ronde to talk to about his feelings.

"It helped tremendously to have someone as close as he was to me in the same industry," said Tiki.[1]

Brown made the most of his opportunity, running for 100 yards six times on his way to a 1,000-yard season. Despite four wins to close out the year, the Giants could not dig themselves out of the hole they created by losing 6 of 8 in the middle of the season. They finished with an 8–8 record, and it did not look like Barber would play a big role in their future plans.

TEAM PLAYER

Barber made only one start in the 1999 season. He was mostly used as a third-down back and special teams player. It was exactly the role his critics thought he would play when he was drafted in 1997. And it was exactly the label Barber wanted to avoid. But he remained a team player and contributed wherever and whenever the opportunity presented itself.

TIKI IN THE SPOTLIGHT

After the 1999 season, Tiki Barber landed a role in an off-Broadway play called *Seeing Double* at the New Amsterdam Café in New York. The play was about twins. Barber enjoyed being on stage, and, by most accounts, put on a solid performance. He said being in a play was a bit like being a football player.

"In acting you have to know other people's lines," Barber said. "Most people don't think about that in football, but you have to know what all your teammates are supposed to do."

"(Tiki) had a stage presence," said producer Stasea Rosenblum, who also starred in the play alongside twin Sheri. "We wish we had 10 of him. He was easy to work with."

Later, Barber performed in other plays, including *Women of Manhattan*.

He did not get many opportunities to carry the football. In fact, he caught more passes (66) than he had rushing attempts (62). He did a little bit of everything, though. He returned kickoffs and punts, and when the season was done, he had piled up some impressive overall numbers. He accumulated 1,639 all-purpose yards, which ranked fourth on the Giants' all-time list at the time.

Barber's two best games came against Dallas. He played a pivotal role in the first game, a 13–10 victory, by returning a punt 85 yards for a touchdown and setting up the game-winning field goal with a 53-yard reception. The Giants lost the season finale at Dallas, but Barber shined by setting a team record with 13 receptions for 100 receiving yards. It was his first career 100-yard receiving game.

The Giants failed to make the playoffs again, however. After winning 5 of its first 8 games, New York fizzled down the stretch with 6 losses in 8 games for a 7–9 overall record.

The big problem was scoring points. The Giants were held to fewer than 20 points in 11 of their 16 games. They finished in the bottom third of the league in scoring. If they were going to be a playoff team in the future, they needed to find a way to get better on offense. What they soon learned, however, was the answer was not a hot free agent. The answer was already on the team. All they had to do was give the ball to the "fiery-tempered king."

Barber celebrates a touchdown against the Cowboys in 1999.

CHAPTER SEVEN

A Super Season

In the 2000 NFL Draft, the New York Giants used the No. 11 pick to select running back Ron Dayne, the Heisman Trophy winner from the University of Wisconsin. The chances of Tiki Barber getting many carries looked about as slim as the Giants' chances of going to the Super Bowl.

But the 2000 season was a year of change. Coach Jim Fassel gave the play-calling duties to offensive coordinator Sean Payton, and Payton had a plan. Instead of using Dayne on running plays and Barber on passing plays, Payton wanted to use both backs. It was the birth of "Thunder and Lightning"—the nickname given to New York's backfield.

Most people thought "thunder" meant Dayne because he was a 250-pound wrecking ball of a back, and Barber was "lightning" because of his speed. But really those names were used by the Giants' coaches to determine which set of players would be on the field. The nickname was catchy, though, so it stuck.

But few people believed the Giants were going to be much of a factor in 2000.

"The experts saw last year and last year we were 7–9," said standout cornerback Jason Sehorn. "Why would you think we were going anywhere? We had a bunch of players that people thought were too old, a quarterback (Kerry Collins) nobody had faith in and a defense that complained too much. So why would anyone expect us to do a lot?"[1]

Barber breaks free for a long run against the Pittsburgh Steelers.

The expectations may have been low, but that all changed in a hurry. The Giants stormed into the season with a 21–16 victory against the Arizona Cardinals. Barber was amazing. He ran for 144 yards—the most ever by a Giant on opening day—and scored 2 touchdowns.

The next week, Barber ran for 96 yards and scored another touchdown in a 33–18 win against the Philadelphia Eagles. "Thunder and Lightning" was in full force. Dayne had run for 128 yards in the first two games, and defenses did not know which way to turn.

"They make it hard to get a bead on what they're going to do," said Eagles' defensive end Hugh Douglas after the game. "Everything looks like the other thing. They make the pass look like run and vice versa."[2]

That was exactly Payton's plan.

"We wanted to make it so there is no alert that it's just pass when Tiki is in the game," said Payton.[3]

Payton's plan worked again the next week against the Chicago Bears. Barber scored for the third straight game on a neatly designed play. While left guard Glenn Parker pulled to his left to draw the Bears defenders his way, Barber skirted to the right and pranced into the end zone. It was a key score as the Giants won 14–7.

Two straight losses snapped New York's fast start. But the Giants got back on track in a hard-fought 13–6 win against the Falcons in Atlanta.

> **"We wanted to make it so there is no alert that it's just pass when Tiki is in the game."**
>
> **—Sean Payton**

That win ignited a four-game winning streak that included key divisional victories against the Dallas Cowboys (19–14) and Philadelphia Eagles (24–7).

Giants fans were really getting excited now. The team was playing great football, but its toughest test was coming up: the defending Super Bowl champion St. Louis Rams. The Rams had a fantastic offense, even without injured starting quarterback Kurt Warner and running back Marshall Faulk. Though the Giants battled hard, they could not stop the Rams. St. Louis won 38–24. It was the most points New York had given up all season.

Barber scored his fifth touchdown of the year—on a 13-yard pass from Collins—and piled up 93 yards from scrimmage, giving him more than 1,000 yards from scrimmage in only the eleventh game of the year.

The Giants could not feel too bad about losing to the Rams. They were the defending champs after all. But a loss the next week to the Detroit Lions made for two straight home defeats and put New York at 7–4 with five games to play. People were starting to

Barber lands in the end zone for a touchdown past Chicago
Bears safety Tony Parrish September 17, 2000.

wonder what kind of team New York had. Were the
Giants a team capable of winning three and four
straight, or were they the team that suffered back-to-
back losses twice? Their coach had the answer.

THIS TEAM IS GOING TO THE PLAYOFFS

The week after the loss to the Lions, Fassel was peppered with questions from the media. He decided the time was right to make a stand.

"I'm raising the stakes right now," the coach said. "If this is a poker game, I'm shoving my chips to the middle of the table. I'm raising the ante. Anybody that wants in, get in. Anybody that wants out can get out."[4]

The press wondered where he was going with this unusual declaration. Then Fassel uttered the words that became the signature of the 2000 Giants.

"This team is going to the playoffs," he said. "This team is going to the playoffs."[5]

The room fell silent for a moment. Did that really just happen? Did the coach of the New York Giants just guarantee his team, which was on a two-game losing streak, would go to the playoffs?

GUARANTEEING VICTORY

Giants coach Jim Fassel's guarantee that his team would make the playoffs made a lot of headlines, but it wasn't the most famous guarantee by a New York sports figure. That happened three days before Super Bowl III in 1969 when New York Jets quarterback Joe Namath told the media, "We're going to win Sunday. I guarantee it." The Jets were 17-point underdogs to the Baltimore Colts, but Namath and the Jets lived up to the guarantee with a shocking 16–7 victory.

When it sunk in, the writers and TV cameramen knew they had the story of the year. It was one thing for a player to guarantee a win. It happens so much that it hardly means anything. But for a coach to make such a statement with five games to go, this was big. The video clip was replayed again and again on ESPN.

"Everybody in the world thought Jim had lost his mind," said Giants' defensive end Michael Strahan. "They figured the Giants, after losing back-to-back games, had gone crazy. It even shocked us—the players—that our coach would stick his neck out so far. We all got caught up in a really positive spirit."[6]

Barber breaks away from Pittsburgh's Levon Kirkland (99) and Chad Scott (30) and runs for 23 yards.

Fassel's tactic worked to perfection. The Giants got hot, real hot. First was a road win against the Arizona Cardinals. Barber had 84 yards from scrimmage and a touchdown. Next was a road game

NEW YORK GIANTS 2000 SEASON

Opponent	W/L	Score
vs Arizona Cardinals	W	21–16
at Philadelphia Eagles	W	33–18
at Chicago Bears	W	14–7
vs Washington Redskins	L	16–6
at Tennessee Titans	L	28–14
at Atlanta Falcons	W	13–6
vs Dallas Cowboys	W	19–14
vs Philadelphia Eagles	W	24–7
at Cleveland Browns	W	24–3
vs St. Louis Rams	L	38–24
vs Detroit Lions	L	31–21
at Arizona Cardinals	W	31–7
at Washington Redskins	W	9–7
vs Pittsburgh Steelers	W	30–10
at Dallas Cowboys	W	17–13
vs Jacksonville Jaguars	W	28–25
PLAYOFFS		
vs Philadelphia Eagles	W	20–10
vs Minnesota Vikings	W	41–0
SUPER BOWL XXXV		
vs Baltimore Ravens	L	34–7

against the Redskins. The Giants had played well and clung to a 9–7 lead in the final moments as Washington sent out kicker Eddie Murray for the game-winning kick.

Then, magically, as if Fassel's guarantee influenced the kick, the ball missed its mark, and the New York Giants won. People began to sense that something special was brewing.

A 30–10 win against the Pittsburgh Steelers made the Giants 10–4 and in great shape to make the playoffs. The following week brought another thrilling win at Dallas. The 17–13 triumph was dampened, however, as Barber suffered a broken left forearm.

Many players would sit out until the injury healed. But Barber had come too far and worked too hard to earn his position to be denied. The last game was a home game against the Jacksonville Jaguars. A win meant New York would play all of its playoff games at home. So, with a cast protecting his broken arm, Barber suited up and played.

Broken arm and all, Barber played great. He scored the game's first touchdown on a 3-yard run in the first quarter. But the Jaguars played determined and built a 10–7 lead going into the fourth quarter. The valiant Giants kept charging and scored 3 touchdowns in the final quarter to post a 28–25 victory. The win made New York 12–4 on the year and the No. 1 seed in the NFC Playoffs.

As the coach had said, this team was going to the playoffs.

Barber ran for 78 yards in the regular-season finale and topped 100 yards from scrimmage. That gave him 1,006 rushing yards on the season—his first 1,000-yard season. He also became the first Giant to top 2,000 all-purpose yards in a season with 2,085.

"Tiki—I've seen it written and I can't argue with—is our most valuable player on offense and maybe as a team. He's had a tremendous year," Fassel said.[7]

THE PLAYOFFS

The Giants had earned a bye in the first round of the playoffs. Tiki rooted for Ronde's Buccaneers in their Wildcard game against the Eagles. But Philadelphia won, preventing a potential matchup of brother vs. brother in the playoffs. It also meant the Giants would play the Eagles for the third time that season.

Barber escapes from Kansas City's Kendrell Bell.

> **"Tiki—I've seen it written and I can't argue with—is our most valuable player on offense and maybe as a team. He's had a tremendous year."**
>
> **—Jim Fassel**

Giants Stadium was rocking when their rivals took the field for the divisional round game. Before the fans could even sit down, Ron Dixon returned the opening kickoff 97 yards for a 7–0 lead.

Both teams played hard on defense, and it was a defensive play that broke the game open. In the second quarter, Philadelphia quarterback Donovan McNabb tried to throw to the outside, but Sehorn made a spectacular play by tipping the pass, rolling, and catching it. He got up and sprinted 32 yards for a touchdown to make the score 17–0.

A late touchdown pass by McNabb made the final score of 20–10 look closer than the game really was. The Giants were never really threatened. Barber only gained 35 yards rushing, but his willingness to play with a broken arm served as inspiration to his teammates to play even harder.

Next up was the NFC Championship against the high-scoring Minnesota Vikings, which included quarterback Daunte Culpepper and all-world wide receiver Randy Moss. It was not even close. The Giants played their finest game of the season and one of the best in franchise history. Collins threw 5 touchdown passes—2 to Ike Hilliard—as New York demolished the Vikings 41–0.

The Giants were going to the Super Bowl.

SUPER BUMMER

The Giants rode a wave of momentum into Super Bowl XXXV at Raymond James Stadium in Tampa, Florida, but they faced a team that was nothing like

Giants quarterback Kerry Collins looks up during the first quarter of Super Bowl XXXV January 28, 2001, in Tampa, Florida.

any they had played before. The AFC Champion Baltimore Ravens had a modest offense but an incredible defense. They had led the league in takeaways with 49 and had allowed the fewest points ever in a 16-game season. To this day, an argument can be made that the 2000 Baltimore defense was the best of all time.

The worst situation for New York developed as the Ravens scored first on a 38-yard touchdown pass from Trent Dilfer to Brandon Stokley in the first quarter. Trailing the Ravens with their nasty defense was no place a team wanted to be.

The Giants seemed to have pulled the momentum back in their favor when linebacker Jessie Armstead intercepted a pass and returned it 43 yards for a touchdown, but the play was called back on a heartbreaking holding penalty. The play would have tied the score at 7.

HARD-HITTING RAY

Baltimore Ravens linebacker Ray Lewis was named MVP of Super Bowl XXXV. Tiki Barber said Lewis is the hardest hitter he has ever played against. "It's a matter of simple physics: Force equals mass times acceleration," said Barber. "He's a big guy at 250 pounds and just as fast as most running backs in the league. When you add those two things together, his mass and acceleration, it's a pretty powerful force."

The Ravens added another field goal, and the Giants were having a tough time gaining yards. Barber finally broke free for a 27-yard run that put New York in position to get points before halftime. But Collins threw one of his 4 interceptions of the game to end the threat.

In the third quarter, Baltimore cornerback Duane Starks returned an interception for a touchdown and a 17–0 lead. Then the fireworks really happened. Dixon returned the kickoff 97 yards for a touchdown. The Giants had life.

But just as quickly as the Giants got back into the game, the Ravens struck back. Jermaine Lewis returned the ensuing kickoff 84 yards for a touchdown. That pushed the Ravens' lead back to 17 at 24–7 and broke the Giants' backs. Three touchdowns on 3 straight plays set a Super Bowl record.

When it was all over, Baltimore had a 34–7 victory. It was a frustrating end to a great season for the Giants. The New York players felt they had not played their best game. With a broken arm and facing such a powerful defense, Barber did about as well as could be expected. He ran for 49 yards and caught 6 passes for 26 yards.

Sure, Barber was disappointed. But it was not his nature to dwell on opportunities missed. Instead, he looked to the future and becoming an even better football player.

CHAPTER EIGHT

Ronde's Turn

8

The emotional letdown of losing a Super Bowl is tough for a team to overcome. It is a long wait until the next season and a chance to erase the memory of being so close to wearing a Super Bowl ring.

For Tiki Barber, the wait was even longer. He suffered a broken bone in his left hand during 2001 training camp and was forced to miss all of the Giants' preseason games. He made it back in time for the opener, but the magic of New York's 2000 season was gone.

The Giants started the season 3–1, but back-to-back one-point losses to the St. Louis Rams and Philadelphia Eagles in weeks 5 and 6 set the tone for the season: The Giants were a decent team, nothing more. They finished the year 7–9 and missed the playoffs.

Kerry Collins (5) watches
Barber carry the ball.

Barber, who missed two games with a hamstring injury, made 9 starts and finished the year with a team-high 865 rushing yards. He caught a career-high 72 passes and accounted for 1,782 total yards, but in the end, the year was a disappointment.

Ronde, on the other hand, had the best year of his career. During his first four years in the league, Ronde had 6 total interceptions. In 2001, however, it seemed that every time the other team threw the ball, Ronde was there. Against New Orleans, he set a Buccaneers record with 3 interceptions. He finished the season with 10 interceptions, tying Cleveland's Anthony Henry for most in the league, and was voted to his first Pro Bowl.

Like 2000, however, Tampa Bay could not get past the Eagles. The Buccaneers lost at Philadelphia 31–9 in a Wildcard Playoff game. It was the second straight season the Eagles knocked the Buccaneers out in the first round.

TIKI TOPS IN THE CONFERENCE

Tiki Barber had a great year individually in 2002 with 1,387 rushing yards and 11 touchdowns. He became the first Giant to lead the NFC in scrimmage yards (1,984 yards) since 1970. New York made the playoffs in 2002 with a 10–6 record but saw a 24-point lead vanish in a 39–38 Wildcard round loss to the San Francisco 49ers.

RONDE'S DREAM COMES TRUE

Before the 2002 season, Tampa Bay fired popular coach Tony Dungy. They replaced him by swinging a trade with the Oakland Raiders to obtain coach Jon Gruden in exchange for four draft picks and $8 million in cash.

It was a lot to pay for a coach, but Gruden was known for working wonders with the Raiders' offense. If the Bucs were going to get past Philly, they would need more than their outstanding defense.

The trade paid off. Tampa Bay won 7 of its first 9 games and finished the regular season with a 12–4 record, good enough for the second seed in the

Jon Gruden (second from right) during his first press conference as head coach of the Tampa Bay Buccaneers

NFC Playoffs. The team was still led by its staunch defense, including Ronde, defensive tackle Warren Sapp, defensive end Simeon Rice, linebacker Derrick Brooks, and safety John Lynch. But the offense was improved. Quarterback Brad Johnson thrived in Gruden's offense, throwing 22 touchdowns with only 6 interceptions.

The Buccaneers routed the San Francisco 49ers 31–6 in the Divisional Round of the playoffs. Tampa Bay's No. 1-ranked defense forced 5 turnovers. The next stop was the NFC Championship game and a meeting with the Philadelphia Eagles.

The Buccaneers had lost three straight to the Eagles and had never won a playoff game on the road, but they were determined this was their year.

It seemed this game was going to be like the others, however. Philadelphia's Brian Mitchell returned the opening kickoff 70 yards to set up a 20-yard scoring run by Duce Staley for a quick 7–0 Eagles lead. But the Bucs kept fighting.

One of the biggest plays in the game came in the first quarter. Johnson hit receiver Joe Jurevicius for a 71-yard completion that set up a one-yard touchdown run by Mike Alstott for a 10–7 lead. The Buccaneers' defense, finally, would play Philadelphia with the lead. It was also a very emotional play because Jurevicius' infant son, Michael, had died earlier in the week. Michael, like Tiki and Ronde, was born prematurely.

RONDE'S HEART SHINES THROUGH

Tyler Gardiner, an eleven-year old from Massillon, Ohio, was like many children. He loved football, and he loved playing video games. He would often use Ronde Barber when playing the games and grew to idolize the Tampa Bay star.

But, unlike most children, Tyler was very sick. He suffered from cancer. Dealing with the extensive treatments for the disease was a part of life for Tyler. While playing in the 2005–06 Pro Bowl in Hawaii, Ronde heard about Tyler's dream of meeting him. In February of 2006, Ronde helped make Tyler's dream come true.

Thanks to donations, Tyler and his family traveled to Tampa. Ronde treated the Gardiners to a tour of the Buccaneers' facility and showered them with signed memorabilia. The biggest gift was Ronde's cleats from the Pro Bowl game, which he also signed.

The day ended with a pizza party. While Tyler and his family appreciated the gifts, it was Ronde's willingness to spend time with them and make Tyler feel special that mattered the most.

"It was really cool. That's all I have to say," Tyler said at the end of day. "This keeps my mind off bad things. This, and watching a football game."

On May 12, 2006, after battling the disease for three and a half years, Tyler died.

Joe Jurevicius and his wife, Meagan, had been through a terrible experience, and it was only fitting that Joe would make the big play to get his team rolling.

In the third quarter, Ronde snuffed out an Eagles drive by sacking quarterback Donovan McNabb and forcing a fumble. Later in the quarter, when Martin Gramatica kicked a 27-yard field goal, the Bucs had a

20–10 lead. That meant Philadelphia was going to have to score twice in the final quarter. There was no way Tampa Bay's defense would allow it.

In the closing moments, the Eagles advanced deep into Buccaneers territory. A touchdown would make for a tense ending. McNabb dropped back to pass and threw for receiver Antonio Freeman. The ball was caught—but not by Freeman. Racing down the sideline was Ronde. He intercepted the pass and ran 92 yards for a touchdown to seal the game. He could have run all the way to San Diego, California—the site of Super Bowl XXXVII.

Naturally, Tiki was there in Veterans Stadium to cheer on his brother.

"I tried the whole game to get on the sideline, but being a New York Giant in Philadelphia, there was no way they were going to let me on the sideline," Tiki said with a laugh.[1]

Fortunately, Tiki ran into the Fox Sports crew.

"Terry Bradshaw said, 'I'm not going out on the sideline anymore. Here take my pass,'" Tiki said.[2]

Tiki and Ronde gave each other a huge hug after the 27–10 victory. For the second time in three years, a Barber was going to the Super Bowl.

In a strange twist of fate, Tampa Bay's Super Bowl opponent was the Raiders, the team they traded with to obtain Gruden. But the Super Bowl was no match. The Buccaneers defense overwhelmed Oakland's passing game, led by league MVP, quarterback Rich Gannon.

In the end, the Bucs picked off Gannon five times in a 48–22 rout. Ronde and the defense were terrific, scoring three times off interceptions.

Ronde was a champion.

Tiki was extremely proud of his brother. He knew how hard Ronde had worked to become an elite player. They are each other's biggest supporters. Of course, Ronde having a Super Bowl ring meant that Tiki was going to work extra hard in the future—to equal his brother's success.

THE 20-20 CLUB

Ronde Barber is one of only seven players in NFL history to intercept 20 passes and record 20 sacks. He is the only defensive back to accomplish the feat. His career totals entering the 2006 season were 28 interceptions, 20 sacks, and 577 tackles.

"He is a pro football player if ever there was one," said Tampa Bay coach Jon Gruden. "He is an undisputed, inspiring leader and a great, clutch performer. He is a very instinctive, physical football player who can cover and play the running game very physically. He is always on the details. He is a great person and a Pro Bowl cornerback."

BROTHER VS. BROTHER

The 2003 season did not turn out as either the Giants or Buccaneers had hoped. Neither made the playoffs. In Week 12, however, Tiki and Ronde squared off against each other as the Giants traveled to Florida to take on the Buccaneers. The teams had met twice since the Barbers were drafted in 1997, but that was before either

Tiki or Ronde had become stars. This was the first game in which they played meaningful roles against each other.

Of course, it was not the first time they had lined up on opposite sides. Tiki and Ronde had practiced against each other many times through the years. But they would always go easy on each other. Early in their college careers at Virginia, a play in practice called for Tiki to block Ronde low, near the knees—a dangerous type of block. Tiki simply gave Ronde a light push instead.

When Tiki was asked by the running backs coach if he thought his brother would do the same, Tiki said, "I know he would."[3]

He was right. Just a few plays later, Ronde had a chance to land a hard tackle on Tiki but just pushed him out of bounds.

RONDE BARBER'S CAREER STATS

YEAR	TACKLES	ASSISTS	SACKS	INTS	YARDS —	TDS	PASSES DEFENDED
1997	4	0	0	0	0	0	0
1998	69	12	3	2	67	0	8
1999	61	16	1	2	60	0	17
2000	73	14	5.5	2	46	1	10
2001	58	13	1	10	86	1	14
2002	67	12	3	2	9	0	17
2003	79	18	1.5	2	53	1	3
2004	83	15	3	3	23	0	10
2005	83	16	2	5	105	0	15
2006	84	14	0	3	103	2	13
TOTAL	661	130	20	31	552	5	107

In the pros, however, the Barbers had no choice but to hit each other hard. During the Week 12 game, a play developed that put Tiki in Ronde's sights.

"He smacked me. He hit me hard," said Tiki. "I was getting tackled. He didn't have to but he came up and drilled me. I said, 'What's up, bro?' He said, 'I'm doing my job.'"[4]

Tampa Bay won the game, 19–13.

END OF AN ERA

The Giants finished 2003 with a miserable 4–12 record and lost eight straight games to close out the season. The fans were growing restless. The Super Bowl season of 2000 seemed a distant memory. Tiki, however, enjoyed another fine season, topping 1,000 yards rushing for a second straight year. He really did it all for New York's offense. He led the team in rushing (1,216 yards) and receptions (69).

With two games to play, the team fired coach Jim Fassel. The Giants players wondered what the future would bring. Tiki had established himself as a team leader, but he had developed a fumbling problem. He fumbled 17 times between 2002 and 2003. Would the new coach, whoever that would be, hold that against him?

It seemed the future was filled with more questions than answers.

CHAPTER NINE

More Than a Football Player

While Tiki Barber's career on the football field was blossoming, his life outside of football was equally important to him. His fame on the football field opened a lot of doors. For instance, if he wanted to dine in New York, all he had to do was call and say, "We're coming," and a table would be waiting.

With that kind of fame, it would be easy to become big-headed and feel more important than the average person. But Geraldine Barber did not raise her sons that way. Tiki viewed his celebrity status as an even better means of giving back.

Charity has always been important to Tiki and Ronde. Tiki has done TV commercials to raise

Barber poses with fans at New York's Murry Bergtraum High School. He helped dedicate the school's sports field.

awareness of a variety of causes and has lent his voice for radio commercials many times, as well.

He supports the Children's Miracle Network through Tiki Barber's 21 Club, which raises funds based on his performance on the field, and supports art education. He holds an annual Tiki Barber Invitational Golf Tournament and always participates in the team's Giants Foundation Golf Outing—both for charity.

Tiki has been involved with programs designed to fight breast cancer, autism, muscular dystrophy, domestic violence, and many others. When a charitable cause calls, Tiki always answers. His wife, Ginny, is also involved in many civic causes.

In fact, Tiki and Ginny have gone to Israel as guests of former Prime Minister Shimon Peres. The trip was not intended to be a mission necessarily, but Tiki visited the Peres Center for Peace, which works at establishing peace in the Middle East and uniting Israelis and Palestinians.

Tiki was greeted by children eager to see an NFL football player even though they knew little about the game. He showed them how to throw a football and told them stories that stressed cooperation and understanding.

"I'd like to work toward providing young people and older people with opportunities to see something else, allowing them to have ideas in their heads they never would have thought about," Tiki said.[1]

SPIN THAT WHEEL, TIKI

Tiki Barber has twice participated in "NFL Players Week" on the *Wheel of Fortune* game show. Many charities have benefited from the annual event, which started in 1997. In 2001, Tiki won $10,000 for the Starlight Children's Foundation. He won another $10,000 in 2002 for Verizon Reads. *Wheel of Fortune* star Vanna White has been a Verizon Literacy Champion since 2001.

Barber meets with Shimon Peres in Tel Aviv, Israel, June 28, 2005. Barber was in Israel as a guest of the Peres Peace Center.

TIKI AND RONDE: AUTHORS

Tiki found another avenue to give back: children's books. The idea of Tiki and Ronde writing a children's book actually came from a child. An editor's son at Simon & Schuster Children's Publishing was a fan of Tiki and made the suggestion that the company do a book with the Barbers. The editors liked the idea and called the Barbers in 2003. Tiki and Ronde embraced the idea right away. It was a natural fit.

Tiki and Ronde grew up loving books thanks to their mother. She always kept books around the house for them to read. In fact, Ronde remembers being able to read before the first grade. When Tiki and Ronde became professional football players, they wanted to help youngsters learn to love reading and writing as they had.

The Barbers became involved with the National Education Association and were named Literacy Champions for the Virginia Literacy Foundation, an organization designed to end illiteracy in Virginia.

"I believe one of the best things we can do is bring attention to the cause of literacy and encourage others to get involved," said Ronde.[2]

DID YOU KNOW?

- Tiki and Ronde Barber have both been selected to *People Magazine's* "50 Most Beautiful People" list.

- Tiki's favorite movie is *The Goonies*.

- Tiki's favorite book is *Harry Potter*.

- Tiki's favorite TV show is *24*.

- Tiki's favorite musician is Lenny Kravitz.

- Tiki's favorite food is kobe steak.

- Tiki said that if he could share dinner with someone who has passed away, he would choose Hall of Fame running back Walter Payton, who died of liver disease in 1999.

- When Tiki went to college, he originally wanted to be an aerospace engineer so he could become an astronaut.

- For a while, Tiki took up boxing in the off-seasons to build up his conditioning.

"The stories were easy because they were true stories that happened and once we decided to do it, the stories were just there."

—Tiki Barber

Tiki and Ronde have been involved in similar causes in New York and Tampa. So, the idea of them writing children's books seemed like the logical next step. Figuring out what the stories would be about actually ended up being no problem at all.

"The stories were easy because they were true stories that happened and once we decided to do it, the stories were just there," said Tiki.[3]

The first book, *By My Brother's Side*, which was published in 2004, told the story of a summertime bicycle accident Tiki had that injured his knee and made him doubt whether he would play sports again. With his brother as motivation, he overcomes the setback to recover in time for football season.

The Barbers wanted the message of the book to stress the importance of family, the importance of never giving up, and to believe in yourself. The book was a huge success and was followed up in 2005 with another book called *Game Day*.

In *Game Day*, the storyline has Ronde playing second fiddle to Tiki, who scores all the touchdowns. In the end, the team needs to score and surprises its opponent by having Tiki throw the ball to Ronde, who scores the winning touchdown.

The Barbers changed the action a bit for a more dramatic ending. In real life, Tiki says, "it wasn't as poetic as it seems. Instead of me getting the ball, getting hit and throwing it to him, it was more he kind of just took my role from the beginning (of the play), and I took his role."[4]

The effect was the same, and the message of how hard work can pay off came through loudly. The books, filled with colorful pictures, have become so popular that a third, titled *Teammates*, was released the day Tiki's Giants host Ronde's Buccaneers during the 2006 season. And there has been talk of an animated show based on the books.

The Barbers have read their books to schoolchildren to encourage reading. The books have also been used in charity auctions. Tiki and Ronde have never forgotten their goals and always make time for children, as was the case at Liberty Elementary School in Sallisaw, Oklahoma. The students there were recognized for their reading achievement with a special surprise package from Tiki and Ronde. It contained two autographed books, an autographed football, and other items.

"I was shocked when I opened the box and saw the things they had sent to us," said Geneva Ford, the Liberty Elementary reading program coordinator. "To see pro athletes recognize boys and girls that set reading goals and then work to meet those goals is such a thrill. So many boys and girls look up to pro athletes. To have a positive response like this is so encouraging."[5]

HEY, THAT'S TIKI ON TV

With their success on the field, Tiki and Ronde had become well-known on the national sports scene. But their popularity exploded with a comical Visa check card commercial that showed a confused sales clerk trying to figuring out which brother was which. The commercial was rerun with a different, yet still comical, ending when Ronde's Buccaneers made the

MEDIA FRIENDLY

Tiki and Ronde Barber were both selected to the NFL All-Interview Team after the 2005 season by NFL.com national editor Vic Carucci. The award goes to players who handle themselves with class regardless if their team wins or loses. It was Tiki's third time being named to the team and Ronde's second. Both Barbers were selected in 2003.

Of Tiki, *The Sporting News'* Dan Pompei said, "He's a true professional with the media and an example for every player in the NFL."

Barber mingles with other stars at a cancer benefit.

Super Bowl after the 2002 season. With that, the Barbers were no longer just sports stars. They were stars, and everybody loved them.

Tiki has since built an impressive media career. Aside from guest appearances on shows such as *All My Children*, *Martha*, *The Apprentice*, and *The Jamie Kennedy Experiment*, he is a regular on *Fox & Friends*. Tiki teamed with New York Giants team treasurer Jonathan Tisch to interview NFL Commissioner Paul Tagliabue, and he even had a lunch interview with Secretary of State Condoleezza Rice.

Tiki has also done radio work for ESPN and has become a regular on Sirius Satellite Radio. He and Ronde host a talk show together called *The Barber Shop*, and Tiki hosts *Tiki Barber's National Sweep*. The *National Sweep* is a news talk show during which Tiki talks about many things outside of sports, such as news, politics, and entertainment.

When Tiki's football playing days are done, he will probably have an easy time finding a job in TV or radio, whether it is in sports or not. That is not an accident. Tiki has always worked hard to be a well-rounded person, not just a good football player. Whatever field he chooses to go into, there is little doubt he will give it the same effort he did in becoming one of pro football's best players.

CHAPTER TEN

Untouchable Tiki

10

On January 6, 2004, the New York Giants met their new head coach, Tom Coughlin. Former coach Jim Fassel was known as a player's coach. That meant he was chummy with his players. It was clear from the first day that things would be different under Coughlin.

Coughlin, who coached the expansion Jacksonville Jaguars to within a game of the Super Bowl in only their second season, explained to the Giants how things would be under his watch. He expected to win.

"We are going to be a disciplined team and the thing that I found interesting is that he sees discipline not as a punitive measure but something that is going to help us win," said Tiki Barber of the initial meeting.[1]

Giants quarterback Eli Manning (10) hands off to Barber in a game against Washington December 5, 2004.

The Giants also added another new part to their team during the 2004 NFL Draft, Mississippi quarterback Eli Manning—the younger brother of All-Pro Peyton Manning. Eli was selected No. 1 overall by the San Diego Chargers despite saying he did not want to play for them. The Giants had the No. 4 pick and selected North Carolina State quarterback Phillip Rivers. Not long after, New York sent Rivers and several draft picks to San Diego in exchange for Eli.

New York released starter Kerry Collins and added former league MVP Kurt Warner as well as more than twenty other veteran players before training camp. The team was definitely taking on a new look. But how would Barber fit in?

PROBLEM SOLVED

Coughlin knew Barber was a tremendous runner and could continue on the success he had had the last few years, but Barber's fumbling problem needed to be fixed. During training camp, Coughlin worked hard with Barber to rethink the way he carried the ball. Barber did drills—over and over again—until the new method became second nature.

"It's amazing sometimes when I look at old videos of myself," said Barber. "It's amazing I didn't fumble more with how loosely I carried the football. (Coach Coughlin) forced me to work on technique, (to hold the ball) high and tight."[2]

GETTING HUGE

Coach Tom Coughlin's drills were a big reason why Tiki Barber cut down on his fumbles, but they were not the only reason. After the Giants lost to the 49ers in a January 2003 playoff game, Barber hooked up with strength trainer Joe Carini. Carini, a six-time New Jersey Strongest Man winner, worked Barber as he had never been worked before. In the off-seasons, Barber usually works out with Carini four times a week. Thanks to the training, Barber has been able to add twenty pounds of muscle and become a faster, stronger runner.

Since Coughlin's arrival in New York, Barber has had 1,170 touches and only 9 fumbles. That is only one fumble for every 130 times he touched the ball.

Yes, Coughlin had his runner all right. And he was definitely going to use him.

TIKI TIME

It became obvious from the first game of 2004 that Coughlin intended to feature his running back. Barber ran for 125 yards and gained 75 more through the air with a touchdown against the Philadelphia Eagles. The Eagles won the game 31–17, but Barber was just getting started.

The Giants reeled off four straight wins, and Barber had 100-yard games in three of them, including a 182-yard effort against Green Bay.

New York's fast start fizzled, however. The passing game went into a bit of a slump. With the team at 5–4 after a 17–14 loss to the Arizona Cardinals, Warner was replaced with Manning.

Manning had a typical rookie beginning to his career. At times he looked like the player the Giants traded so much to get. At other times, he looked like a college quarterback playing against professionals. It all meant that Barber was going to have to shoulder even more of the offense.

Barber was up to the task. He ran for more than 100 yards in each of Manning's first two starts. But the losses were piling up. The low point was a three-week stretch of losses in which the Giants were outscored 95–27 by the Eagles, Redskins, and Ravens.

But then things began to click for Manning. In Week 15, the Giants hosted the Pittsburgh Steelers, who were 12–1 coming into the game. Eli found his rhythm and passed for 182 yards and 2 touchdowns without being sacked. Barber ran for 76 yards and caught 5 passes for 38 yards. His one-yard touchdown run in the fourth quarter gave the Giants a 30–26 lead. Fullback Jim Finn paved the way with a key block as Barber followed him through the right side of the line. It was a gutsy play, as it was fourth down.

Pittsburgh's Jerome Bettis scored the game-winning touchdown with a little more than four minutes to play. The 33–30 loss was disappointing for the Giants since they had played so well. But Giants fans knew the future was looking good.

THE FUTURE IS NOW

After a 23–22 loss to Cincinnati left the Giants with their eighth straight defeat, the team prepared for the season finale against the Dallas Cowboys. The Giants were not going to the playoffs, but there would be no better way to start the 2005 season than to finish 2004 with a victory against their division rivals.

The game was a classic, with each team taking each other's best punches. It appeared the Cowboys

Barber finds his way through a pack of players on a 5-yard touchdown run against the Minnesota Vikings October 31, 2004.

were going to win when Julius Jones scored with 1:49 to play for a 24–21 lead. But Manning drove the Giants down the field for a frantic finish. There were only 11 seconds remaining, and the Giants had the ball at the Cowboys' 3-yard line. Everyone knew Barber would get the ball. Manning handed the ball to Barber, and he pushed his way in for the touchdown and a 28–24 victory.

On the final carry, Barber passed Joe Morris for the single-season Giants rushing record—1,518 yards. Earlier in the game, he passed Rodney Hampton to become the team's all-time leading rusher.

Barber was magnificent in 2004. He led the league with 2,096 yards from scrimmage and was named to his first Pro Bowl. He ran for more than 100 yards in nine games and scored in all but four games, finishing with 15 touchdowns.

With their young quarterback maturing and Barber playing the best football of his career, the Giants were eager for 2005.

TIKI KEEPS GETTING BETTER

In 2005, Barber had one of the finest seasons by anyone—ever—in the NFL. It seemed every time he touched the ball, he set another record. And unlike the year before, the Giants were winning.

Barber played well through the first nine games of the season. He ran for 855 yards and collected 7 touchdowns—6 rushing and one receiving. At that

TEAMMATES AGAIN

Tiki and Ronde Barber became teammates again when they were both selected to play for the NFC in the Pro Bowl after the 2004 season. They became the third pair of brothers to earn such an honor. The others were: Clay and Bruce Matthews and Shannon and Sterling Sharpe. Tiki and Ronde were both chosen for the Pro Bowl again after the 2005 season.

point, however, he kicked into a gear that had to surprise even him. During the next seven games, as the Giants marched their way into the playoffs with an 11–5 record, Barber went absolutely wild.

Barber topped 100 yards in six of the last seven games, gaining 1,005 yards while scoring 4 more touchdowns. His late stretch of production was more than many starting backs had all season.

He topped 200 yards in three different games, becoming only the third player to run for 200 yards three times in a season. Of course, he also did a lot of damage as a receiver. When it was all done, Barber

HOW GOOD WAS TIKI IN 2005?

With three 200-yard rushing games in 2005, Tiki Barber:

* Had more 200-yard games than the rest of the runners in the NFL had the entire season (two).

* Became the third player in NFL history with three 200-yard games in a season.

* Became the first player in NFL history to rush for 1,800 yards and receive for more than 500 in a season.

* Became the fourth player in NFL history with two 200-yard games in a month.

* Became the sixth player in NFL history with four 200-yard games in a career.

* Became the first player in NFL history to gain 200 yards in three games in a single season while carrying the ball less than 30 times in each game; Barry Sanders and Earl Campbell had two 200-yard games in a season with less than 30 carries.

accumulated 2,390 total yards of offense (1,860 rushing and 530 receiving)—the second most for one season in NFL history. He also became the first player to rush for more than 1,800 yards and receive for more than 500.

"Where would we be without him?" asked Giants defensive tackle Kendrick Clancy. "I don't even want to think about it."[3]

Along the way, he set a team record with 220 rushing yards against Kansas City. In that game, he showed his toughness as he trampled through Chiefs along the left sideline on his way to a 41-yard touchdown. In the season finale, he showed his speed on a 95-yard touchdown against the Raiders.

Barber scored 11 touchdowns in 2005, and like his brother Ronde, was voted to his second straight Pro Bowl.

PLAYING FOR MORE THAN HIMSELF

Barber's outrageous statistics only tell part of the 2005 season story. The man behind the stats stands for a lot more than 100-yard games and touchdowns. And his character shined through more than ever when the Giants family needed him.

Prior to the Week 7 home game against the Broncos, the Giants knew their co-owner Wellington Mara was losing his battle with cancer. New York played extra hard for their owner and overcame a 13-point deficit to defeat Denver. Manning, backpedaling away from the line, hit a leaping Amani Toomer for the winning touchdown with only five seconds to play. The 24–23 victory ended up being the last game Mara saw.

The Monday after the game, the Mara family invited Barber and tight end Jeremy Shockey to visit with him. A day later, Mara died.

The following week was extremely emotional for all the Giants. The funeral was held that Friday.

It was a rainy day, but when the Giants stepped onto the practice field later in the day, Barber noticed

NO TIME FOR REST

At the Pro Bowl, most players use the time to relax. Before the 2005 Pro Bowl in Hawaii, however, Tiki Barber got a small taste of military life. Barber, New York City Police Detective Ken Cardona, and a few others were sitting poolside when they were approached by Captain Rob Wolfe of the 2nd Battalion, 35th Infantry based in Hawaii.

After a pleasant conversation, Wolfe invited Barber to run with his troops early one morning. Barber agreed, and when he and the others arrived for the run, they were greeted by 115 men eager to work out with an NFL star. Barber led the early morning run.

"These young guys and their families make great sacrifices every day," said Wolfe. "To have someone like Tiki Barber come here is huge. I can talk and lead and try to motivate them until I'm blue in the face. But to have a professional football player and some of NYPD's finest come here to tell them they believe in what they are doing gives them a sense of purpose that I can't provide."

a hole in the clouds. "There was a beam of sunlight on our practice field, and I said, 'Coach, that's Mr. Mara looking down on us,'" Barber recalled.[4]

The next game was at home against Washington. Fueled by the desire to win for their beloved owner, the Giants ran over the Redskins. Barber was terrific.

Barber dodges cornerback Shawn Springs in a game against the Washington Redskins October 30, 2005.

He dashed through Washington almost at will for 206 yards and nearly scored on a 59-yard run before being tackled at the one-yard line by safety Ryan Clark.

With the flag at Giants Stadium flying at half mast to honor Mara, the day was nearly complete as the Giants led 29–0 in the third quarter. But there was one problem. Barber had promised Mara's grandson Timmy McDonnell that he would score a touchdown.

With the score so lopsided, it was nearly time for Barber to be pulled from the game. With a little less than four minutes to play in the third quarter, the Giants recovered a fumble at the Washington 23. This was it. Barber had to score.

Manning hit Shockey with a pass for a first down that put the ball at the 6-yard line. Barber ran for 2 yards on first down. He was stuffed for no gain on second. It was third-and-goal from the 4. He had to score or the team would be criticized for "rubbing it in" if they went for it instead of kicking the field goal on fourth down.

On the play, Manning turned and handed to Barber for a third straight time. Barber eyed the goal line. He ran with his all power. He ran with all his love. And he powered into the end zone.

Barber ran straight to the sideline where Timmy was waiting and gave him the ball.

A superstar with a super heart—that's Tiki Barber.

CAREER STATISTICS

Rushing

YEAR	TEAM	GAMES	ATTEMPTS	YARDS	AVG	TD
1997	Giants	12	136	511	3.8	3
1998	Giants	16	52	166	3.2	0
1999	Giants	16	62	258	4.2	0
2000	Giants	16	213	1,006	4.7	8
2001	Giants	14	166	865	5.2	4
2002	Giants	16	304	1,387	4.6	11
2003	Giants	16	278	1,216	4.4	2
2004	Giants	16	322	1,518	4.7	13
2005	Giants	16	357	1,860	5.2	9
2006	Giants	16	327	1,662	5.1	5
TOTAL		154	2,217	10,449	4.7	55

Receiving

YEAR	TEAM	GAMES	NUMBER	YARDS	AVG	TD
1997	Giants	12	34	299	8.8	1
1998	Giants	16	42	348	8.3	3
1999	Giants	16	66	609	9.2	2
2000	Giants	16	70	719	10.3	1
2001	Giants	14	72	577	8	0
2002	Giants	16	69	597	8.7	0
2003	Giants	16	69	461	6.7	1
2004	Giants	16	52	578	11.1	2
2005	Giants	16	54	530	9.8	2
2005	Giants	16	58	465	8.0	0
TOTAL		154	586	5,183	8.8	12

Kick returns

YEAR	TEAM	GAMES	NUMBER	YARDS	AVG	TD
1997	Giants	12	0	0	---	0
1998	Giants	16	14	250	17.9	0
1999	Giants	16	12	266	22.2	0
2000	Giants	16	1	28	28	0
2001	Giants	14	0	0	---	0
2002	Giants	16	0	0	---	0
2003	Giants	16	0	0	---	0
2004	Giants	16	0	0	---	0
2005	Giants	16	0	0	---	0
2006	Giants	16	0	0	---	0
TOTAL		154	27	544	20.1	0

Punt returns

YEAR	TEAM	GAMES	NUMBER	YARDS	AVG	TD
1997	Giants	12	0	0	---	0
1998	Giants	16	0	0	---	0
1999	Giants	16	44	506	11.5	1
2000	Giants	16	39	332	8.5	0
2001	Giants	14	38	338	8.9	0
2002	Giants	16	1	5	5	0
2003	Giants	16	0	0	---	0
2004	Giants	16	0	0	---	0
2005	Giants	16	0	0	---	0
2006	Giants	16	0	0	---	0
TOTAL		154	122	1,181	9.7	1

CAREER ACHIEVEMENTS

- New York Giants' all-time leader in rushing attempts (2,217), yards (10,449), and touchdowns (55)

- First player in NFL history to rush for more than 1,800 yards and receive for more than 500 yards in one season (2005)

- Selected for the Pro Bowl three times (2004, 2005, 2006)

- Led the NFL in yards from scrimmage in 2004 (2,096) and 2005 (2,390). The 2005 total was the second most in league history behind Marshall Faulk's 2,429 (1999)

- Ran for more than 200 yards three times in 2005, one more than the rest of the backs in the NFL combined

- Has 17,367 career yards, the most in Giants history

- Is the Giants' all-time leader in receptions with 586
- Is fourth in Giants' history in punt-return yards (1,181)
- Played in Super Bowl XXXV
- Holds Giants' record for single-season receptions by a running back with 72 (2001)
- Graduated from the University of Virginia as the school's all-time leading rusher with 3,389 yards. The record has since been broken by Thomas Jones (3,998)

CHAPTER NOTES

CHAPTER 1. TIKI EQUALS EXCITEMENT

1. Michael Eisen, "Giants Over Raiders, 30–21," giants.com, December 31, 2005, <http://www.giants.com/news/eisen/story.asp?story_id=13005> (May 22, 2006).

2. "Tiki & Ronde Barber to Publish Children's Book," theacc.com, April 9, 2003, <http://www.theacc.com/sports/m-footbl/spec-rel/040903aad.html> (May 23, 2006).

3. Larry Weisman, "Panthers whitewash Giants 23–0, will face Bears next," *USA Today*, January, 9, 2006, <http://www.usatoday.com/sports/football/games/2006-01-08-panthers-giants_x.htm> (June 16, 2006).

4. Ibid.

CHAPTER 2. BROTHERS AND BEST FRIENDS

1. Chris Meyers interview with Tiki Barber, November 20, 2005, <http://msn.foxsports.com/CMI> (June 13, 2006).

2. Jamal Thalji, "A charmed childhood," *St. Petersburg Times*, November 5, 2000, <http://www.sptimes.com/News/110500/Sports/A_charmed_childhood.shtml> (June 1, 2006).

3. Chris Meyers interview with Tiki Barber, November 20, 2005, <http://msn.foxsports.com/CMI> (June 13, 2006).

4. *Readers' Digest* interview with Tiki Barber, May 2006, <http://www.rd.com/content/openContent.do?contentId=26666> (June 3, 2006).

5. Ibid.

CHAPTER 3. MAKING THE GRADE

1. Frank Vehorn, "The Barbers of C'Ville: Identical twins Ronde and Tiki Barber complement each other and U.VA.'s football team—one starring on offense, the other on defense," *The Virginian-Pilot*, October 26, 1996, <http://scholar.lib.vt.edu/VA-news/VA-Pilot/issues/1995/vp951102/11020511.htm> (June 9, 2006).

2. "College Flashback: Tiki Barber," *U.S. News & World Report*, September 8, 2005, <http://www.usnews.com/usnews/edu/college/student-center/flash-back/flashback_090805_brief.php> (May 29, 2006).

3. Nazneen Malik, "Giants' Tiki Barber Supports Art Education," *Education Update*, February 2005, <http://www.educationupdate.com/archives/2005/february/html/Black-Giants.html> (May 25, 2006).

4. Frank Vehorn, "The Barbers of C'Ville: Identical twins Ronde and Tiki Barber complement each other and U.VA.'s football team—one starring on offense, the other on defense," *The Virginian-Pilot*, October 26, 1996, <http://scholar.lib.vt.edu/VA-news/VA-Pilot/issues/1995/vp951102/11020511.htm> (June 9, 2006).

5. Ibid.

6. Ibid.

7. Frank Vehorn, "Coming full circle: He's gone from hero to zero and back in 2 years," *The Virginian-Pilot*, October 24, 1997, <http://scholar.lib.vt.edu/VA-news/VA-Pilot/issues/1997/vp971024/10240687.htm> (June 9, 2006).

CHAPTER 4. PLAYING WITH PRIDE AND PURPOSE

1. Joy Bennett Kinnon, "I Beat Breast Cancer," *Ebony*, October, 2001, <http://www.findarticles.com/p/articles/mi_m1077/is_12_56/ai_78919281> (May 30, 2006).

2. Chris Meyers interview with Tiki Barber, November 20, 2005, <http://msn.foxsports.com/CMI> (June 13, 2006).

3. Joy Bennett Kinnon, "I Beat Breast Cancer," *Ebony*, October, 2001, <http://www.findarticles.com/p/articles/mi_m1077/is_12_56/ai_78919281> (May 30, 2006).

4. Chris Meyers interview with Tiki Barber, November 20, 2005, <http://msn.foxsports.com/CMI> (June 13, 2006).

5. "College Flashback: Tiki Barber," *U.S. News & World Report*, September 8, 2005, <http://www.usnews.com/usnews/edu/college/student-center/flash-back/flashback_090805_brief.php> (May 29, 2006).

CHAPTER 5. INTO THE NFL

1. *Readers' Digest* interview with Tiki Barber, May 2006, <http://www.rd.com/content/openContent.do?contentId=26666> (June 3, 2006).

2. Lisa R. Foeman, "A Mother's Dynamic Duo," MOSAEC, February, 2006, <http://www.mosaec.com/mosaec/sports/sports_barber.htm> (May 30, 2006).

CHAPTER 6. THE ROUGH EARLY YEARS

1. *Readers' Digest* interview with Tiki Barber, May 2006, <http://www.rd.com/content/openContent.do?contentId=26666> (June 3, 2006).

CHAPTER 7. A SUPER SEASON

1. Bob Harig, "No one expected them here," *St. Petersburg Times*, January 21, 2001, <http://www.sptimes.com/News/012101/SuperBowl2001/No_one_expected_them_.shtml> (June 4, 2006).

2. Dan Pompei, "Thunder and Lightning become a flammable mix," *The Sporting News*, September 25, 2000, <http://www.findarticles.com/p/articles/mi_m1208/is_39_224/ai_65730460> (June 7, 2006).

3. Ibid.

4. Ernest Hooper, "The Giants: 10 memorable events," *St. Petersburg Times*, January 26, 2001, <http://www.sptimes.com/News/012601/SuperBowl2001/The_Giants__10_memora.shtml> (June 8, 2006).

5. Ibid.

6. Hubert Mizell, "Attitude is a Giant difference," January 27, 2001, <http://www.sptimes.com/News/012701/SuperBowl2001/Attitude_is_a_Giant_d.shtml> (May 22, 2006).

7. John C. Cotey, "Giants quotebook," *St. Petersburg Times*, January 27, 2001, <http://www.sptimes.com/News/012701/SuperBowl2001/Giants_quote-book_.shtml> (June 9, 2006).

CHAPTER 8. RONDE'S TURN

1. *Readers' Digest* interview with Tiki Barber, May 2006, <http://www.rd.com/content/openContent.do?contentId=26666> (June 3, 2006).

2. Ibid.

3. Frank Vehorn, "The Barbers of C'Ville: Identical twins Ronde and Tiki Barber complement each other and U.VA.'s football team—one starring on offense, the other on defense," *The Virginian-Pilot*, October 26, 1996, <http://scholar.lib.vt.edu/VA-news/VA-Pilot/issues/1995/vp951102/11020511.htm> (June 9, 2006).

4. *Readers' Digest* interview with Tiki Barber, May 2006, <http://www.rd.com/content/openContent.do?contentId=26666> (June 3, 2006).

CHAPTER 9. MORE THAN A FOOTBALL PLAYER

1. Associated Press, "Ex-Israeli PM invited Barber earlier this year," ESPN.com, July 2, 2005, <http://sports.espn.go.com/nfl/news/story?id=2099194> (June 13, 2006).

2. Verizon Literacy Network, "Literacy Champion: The Barber Brothers," June 23, 2003, <http://verizonreads.net/champions/barberbros.asp> (June 16, 2006).

3. *Readers' Digest* interview with Tiki Barber, May 2006, <http://www.rd.com/content/openContent.do?contentId=26666> (June 3, 2006).

4. Ibid.

5. "Students Recognized For Reading Achievement," *Sequoyah County Times*, May 26, 2006, <http://www.sequoyahcountytimes.com/articles/2006/05/26/education/sallisaw_area/7libertysallisaw.txt> (June 16, 2006).

CHAPTER 10. UNTOUCHABLE TIKI

1. ESPN.com, "Coughlin holds first team meeting with Giants," March 22, 2004, <http://sports.espn.go.com/espn/wire?section=nfl&id=1765731> (June 15, 2006).

2. Chris Meyers interview with Tiki Barber, November 20, 2005, <http://msn.foxsports.com/CMI> (June 13, 2006).

3. Clark Judge, "Crime of omission: Tiki getting no love for MVP," CBS SportsLine.com, December 13, 2005, <http://www.cbs.sportsline.com/nfl/story/9094323/1> (June 15, 2006).

4. Chris Meyers interview with Tiki Barber, November 20, 2005, <http://msn.foxsports.com/CMI> (June 13, 2006).

GLOSSARY

cut—To suddenly change direction to lose a pursuing player.

defense—The team defending its goal line. The defense does not have the ball; rather, they attempt to keep the offense from passing or running the ball over their (the defense's) goal line.

defensive back—A member of the defense whose job it is to make tackles, intercept passes, and stop the other team from completing passes. There are usually four defensive backs in a normal defense: two cornerbacks and two safeties.

draft—The selection of new players into the pro ranks from among the various top college players. Teams doing poorly are allowed to choose before those doing well.

free agent—A player whose contract with a team has expired, and the player is able to sign a contract with another team.

Heisman Trophy—An award, named after former college football player and coach John W. Heisman, given to the best player in college football each year.

linebacker—Defensive player placed behind the defensive linemen. The linebacker's job is to tackle runners and block or intercept passes. There are three or four linebackers in a starting lineup.

National Football League (NFL)—The best-known association of professional football teams. Composed of the American Football and National Football conferences, which each have sixteen teams. The champions of each conference play each other in the Super Bowl at the end of each season.

offense—The team with the ball; the offense attempts to run or pass the ball across the defense's goal line.

offensive linemen—The center, two guards, and two tackles. The linemen's job is to block—push the defense back on running plays and protect the quarterback on passing plays.

redshirt—A college athlete who is kept out of varsity competition for a year in order to extend eligibility.

regular season—A time period of seventeen weeks during which a team plays sixteen games to determine its seeding going into the playoffs.

running back—There are two running backs, positioned behind the quarterback, whose job is to run with the ball, typically handed off by the quarterback.

special-teams player—A member of a football team who does not normally play on offense or defense but participates in certain plays such as kickoffs and punts.

spoiler—A team that has no chance of going to the playoffs but can deprive another team of reaching that goal by defeating them.

third-down back—A type of running back, also referred to as a scat back, who usually enters the game when the offense is facing an obvious passing down on third down. This player is usually a small, fast runner who is skilled at pass-catching.

tight end—An offensive player who usually lines up next to the offensive linemen. Sometimes his job is to help the linemen block on running plays. Other times, the tight end goes out to catch passes, like a receiver.

United States Football League—A professional football league that played from 1983 to 1985.

World League of American Football—A professional football league that was backed by the NFL in 1991. It has become the NFL Europe League.

XFL—A professional football league that played only one season (2001).

FOR MORE INFORMATION

FURTHER READING

Barber, Tiki, and Ronde Barber with Robert Burleigh. *By My Brother's Side*. New York: Simon & Schuster/Paula Wiseman Books, 2004.

Barber, Tiki, and Ronde Barber with Robert Burleigh. *Game Day*. New York: Simon & Schuster/Paula Wiseman Books, 2005.

WEB LINKS

Barber's NFL.com page:
http://www.nfl.com/players/playerpage/1782

Barber's page on Giants.com:
http://www.giants.com/team/player.asp?player_id=4

The Giants Foundation:
http://www.giants.com/off_field/TheGiantsFoundation.html

University of Virginia Athletics site:
http://virginiasports.cstv.com/

Verizon Literacy Network:
http://www.verizonreads.net/

INDEX

A

Aikman, Troy, 60

Alstott, Mike, 84

Arizona Cardinals, 68, 73, 103

Armstead, Jessie, 78

Atlanta Falcons, 53, 68, 73

B

Baltimore Ravens, 34, 52, 54, 59, 73, 78–79

Barber, Geraldine, 16, 17, 18, 19, 20–21, 22, 23–24, 25, 26, 27, 28, 39–41, 55, 90, 94

Barber, James, 16, 17

Barber, Ronde, 7, 9, 15, 16, 17, 18, 20, 21–30, 32, 33, 38, 39, 40, 41, 43, 47, 48–49, 50, 52, 54, 55, 63, 75, 82, 84, 85, 86, 87–89, 90, 93–99, 106, 108

Barber, Tiki

as author, 21–22, 93, 95–96

birth of, 16

at Cave Spring High School, 24–25, 27

named academic All-American, 37, 47

named ACC Player of the Year, 47

named Literacy Champion, 94

origin of name, 16–17

in Pro Bowl, 12, 13, 82, 85, 106, 108, 109

track records, 24

at Virginia, 27, 28, 29, 30–38, 39, 40, 41, 43–45, 47

New York Giants

   draft Tiki Barber, 54

O

Oakland Raiders, 5–9, 11, 12, 13, 14, 23, 62, 83, 86–87, 108

P

Payton, Sean, 66, 68

Peres Center for Peace, 92

Peres, Shimon, 92

Philadelphia Eagles, 10, 52, 58–60, 61, 68, 69, 73, 75–76, 80, 82, 84–86, 103, 104

Pittsburgh Steelers, 37, 73, 74, 104

Poindexter, Anthony, 34, 35

R

Reed, Jake, 61

Rice, Condoleezza, 99

Rice, Simeon, 84

Rivers, Phillip, 101

S

St. Louis Rams, 13, 59, 69, 73, 80

San Diego Chargers, 13, 62, 101

San Francisco 49ers, 82, 84, 102

Sapp, Warren, 84

Sehorn, Jason, 67, 76

Sharper, Jamie, 52, 54

Sirius Satellite Radio, 98